RESTIVE PARTNERS

Washington and Bonn Diverge

W. R. Smyser
with a Foreword by Paul H. Nitze

Westview Press
BOULDER, SAN FRANCISCO, & LONDON

Studies in Global Security

This Westview softcover edition is printed on acid-free paper and bound in library-quality, coated covers that carry the highest rating of the National Association of State Textbook Administrators, in consultation with the Association of American Publishers and the Book Manufacturers' Institute.

Published in 1990 in the United States of America by Westview Press, Inc., 5500 Central Avenue, Boulder, Colorado 80301, and in the United Kingdom by Westview Press, 13 Brunswick Centre, London WC1N 1AF, England

Library of Congress Cataloging-in-Publication Data
Smyser, W. R., 1931–
  Restive partners : Washington and Bonn diverge / W. R. Smyser.
    p. cm. — (Studies in global security)
  ISBN 0-8133-7711-0
  1. Germany (West)—Military policy. 2. United States—Military
policy. 3. Germany (West)—Military relations—United States.
4. United States—Military relations—Germany (West). I. Title.
II. Series.
UA710.S526 1990
355′.033543—dc20   89-29016
                                                                         CIP

Printed and bound in the United States of America

⊗ The paper used in this publication meets the requirements of the American National
   Standard for Permanence of Paper for Printed Library Materials Z39.48-1984.

10   9   8   7   6   5   4   3   2   1

RESTIVE PARTNERS

STUDIES IN GLOBAL SECURITY

Alan Ned Sabrosky, Series Editor

Restive Partners: Washington and Bonn Diverge, W. R. Smyser

Defense and Détente: U.S. and West German Perspectives on Defense Policy, Joseph I. Coffey and Klaus von Schubert

The U.S.-Canada Security Relationship: The Politics, Strategy, and Technology of Defense, edited by David G. Haglund and Joel J. Sokolsky

Security in Northeast Asia: Approaching the Pacific Century, edited by Stephen P. Gibert

Alliances in U.S. Foreign Policy: Issues in the Quest for Collective Defense, edited by Alan Ned Sabrosky

Contents

Foreword

For a thousand years, developments in Central Europe have been at the heart of European history and thus of world history. In the latter half of that millennium the basic theme of European history has been the consolidation of powerful nation states dominating areas linked by common geographic, linguistic, and cultural factors. The Germans were the last important geographic and culturally distinctive European group to achieve nationhood. Germany became a nation in 1871 after three brilliant military campaigns that were made possible by Germany's energetic and growing population, its dedication to competence in military-industrial matters, and Otto von Bismarck's exceptional leadership. After the Franco-Prussian War, it was evident that a coalition of almost all of the rest of Europe would be required to offset German military and industrial strength. As demonstrated in the two world wars, even that was not enough. U.S. intervention was necessary in both those wars to swing the balance against Germany.

The peace following World War I was totally mishandled. President Woodrow Wilson's Fourteen Points would have assured a nonpunitive, just, and generous peace. But he was first opposed by the U.S. Senate, then outsmarted by nationalistic and vindictive European political leaders. Wilson became ill and incompetent, leaving a peace that was so palpably unworkable as to bring on a great depression and so vengeful and unjust as to make a second world war unavoidable.

After that second war, Americans gave much study to the causes of the two wars and the errors of the peace concluding World War I. Toward the end of World War II and immediately thereafter, U.S. attention was primarily focused on getting the troops home, converting from war production to normal business pursuits, and maintaining the alliance with the Soviet Union that was forged during the war. Only after two very difficult years, 1945 and 1946, in that latter endeavor did the United States reluctantly conclude that Josef Stalin had no intention of working toward a just and constructive peace in Europe. In February 1947, President Harry Truman, backed by Secretary of State George Marshall and Undersecretary of State Dean Acheson, concluded that the United States must take a much more active political, economic, and, if necessary, military role in containing Soviet expansionism. There quickly followed the Greek-Turkish Aid Program, the Truman Doctrine, the creation of the State Department's Policy Planning Staff, the Marshall Plan, and the passage of the Defense Act of 1947, which created the Defense Department, the Joint Chiefs of Staff, and the Central Intelligence Agency. The U.S. concern was global, but its focus was on Central Europe. The situation in Poland and Czechoslovakia had triggered World War II; Stalin's uncompromising positions concerning Berlin and East Germany, Poland, and Czechoslovakia in 1946 poisoned the prospects for an acceptable peace.

For forty-two years—since 1947—the United States has attempted to create a worldwide system of order—economic, political, and military—against the persistent opposition of the Soviet Union and its satellite regimes. This confrontation has been most comprehensive and enduring in Central Europe and, in particular, in the two Germanys and Berlin.

In the years subsequent to 1947, Britain, France, and the United States unified their zones of occupation in Germany and Berlin. They then supported Chancellor Konrad Adenauer's decision, for the time being, to accept the division of Germany and Berlin and to bring peace and prosperity to the portion of Germany within each country's area of responsibility and control. The resurgence of West Germany has truly been an economic and political miracle. Blocked by the Soviet Union from concluding a peace treaty that would have established a unified Germany, the United States, backed by England and France, strove to bring West Germany into the community of nations. That objective has been fully realized. West Germany is now one of the world's most powerful and most prosperous states. As Richard Smyser emphasizes in this book, West Germany has become a new Germany, with different capabilities and needs than the Germany of Adenauer's days. In this new context, the USSR appears to be evolving into a different USSR. And the United States is a different United States.

Few people in the United States dealt intimately with postwar Germany. General Lucius Clay was originally in command of U.S. military forces. Robert Murphy was his political adviser. Then John J. McCloy became high commissioner, with a small but able staff. In Washington, General William Draper, Deputy Secretary of the Army, devoted himself to German affairs. In the State Department a series of Foreign Service officers of distinction spent much of their lives on German affairs. But with each change of administration there have been shifts in personnel. The new people taking over responsibility for U.S. policy toward Germany have not always been sensitive to what was going on below the surface: the changing attitudes, anxieties, desires, and ambitions of Germans and West Germany. There is, thus, a tremendous need for a book that objectively presents the extraordinary history of the relationship between the Federal Republic of Germany and the United States, the current problems in that relationship, and the opportunities and dangers for that relationship in the future.

The story is complex. Smyser looks closely at the subject of security, including extended deterrence, flexible response, the Strategic Defense Initiative, conventional forces, burden sharing, arms control, and coordination outside of NATO. He then addresses relations with the East, including the "common European home," "Genscherism," and inter-German relations. A third area is the contrasting economic philosophies, in terms of the global economy and the European community and the complementary and divisive tendencies affecting the future of U.S.-German economic relations. Finally, there is a very illuminating discussion of the German wish for reunification. Dr. Smyser deals with all these subjects from an extraordinarily well-informed background. He is one of the few Americans who has followed U.S.-German developments with intimate knowledge and understanding over the years.

If Mikhail Gorbachev's "new look" program is to be achieved, the USSR must develop a new relation of cooperation with West Germany. Significant reduction in Soviet expenditures of resources on its military depends on its success in negotiating equalizing reductions of conventional forces in Europe. Reductions in resources formerly devoted to Soviet military forces can assist *perestroika* if the resources are redirected at modernizing factories that produce civilian goods. West German banks have already lent billions of Deutschmarks to Soviet industries for the purchase of modern plants and equipment. The process is thus even now underway.

As many West Germans see the future, they have closer relations with the USSR and the Central European regimes (including Poland, the GDR, Hungary, and perhaps Czechoslovakia) than the United States and other West European states will have. They see themselves as economically and, potentially, politically stronger than any other continental European power. They are not, therefore, susceptible to the same pressures to which they were once responsive.

Future U.S. relations with West Germany, then, must be based more on independent German judgment than on U.S. pressure on Germany to back U.S. policies. To understand how to design policies that are convergent with German interests requires an understanding of the issues so lucidly set forth in *Restive Partners*.

Paul H. Nitze

Preface

Crashes of U.S. and other allied military jets on West German soil provoke demonstrations and parliamentary debates. Ill-tempered accusations between Washington and Bonn follow the sale of German chemical manufacturing equipment to Libya. The German government firmly promotes arms-control talks just as firmly opposed by Washington. The President of the Soviet Union is more popular in West Germany than the President of the United States. The German central bank raises interest rates and provokes a Wall Street crash. A U.S. Secretary of State is told that the German government will not deploy missiles as he asks.

German-American relations, once the carefully sheltered private province of a few devoted acolytes, whether diplomats, scholars, or soldiers, have become the stuff of headlines and disagreements. The two allies, who have loyally held together the respective ends of the Atlantic alliance through four decades of cold war and crisis, often do not sound or behave as one might expect of friends. A casual observer would have to be forgiven for wondering about the future of that alliance when most of what is heard are arguments.

Those arguments between the Federal Republic of Germany and the United States of America are not made of whole cloth. They are not figments of some journalist's hyperactive imagination. They are not due to personality conflicts. They originate in new and unassimilated realities. The two countries have changed. So has the world around them. So, therefore, has their relationship.

With those changes come dramatic opportunities. The United States and the Federal Republic are among the world's most powerful and most prosperous states. They are at the center of every significant international structure. They have immensely important common interests, even as they argue. If they work together, they can move the entire world in directions that should be not only to their own benefit but to the benefit of all.

If they do not, it is another story.

Recent events suggest that they may not. The two countries are now heading in directions that can at some point create a genuine rift. If that comes, it would come not because it was sought but because it was not energetically avoided. It would come because each government acted without understanding the other's needs, perhaps on the basis of what was best for itself but not on the basis of what was best for the partnership. Each would have done what it thought was right, in dozens if not hundreds of instances. In the process, however, each might have destroyed what was important.

After this manuscript was completed in the fall of 1989, the East German refugee flight to West Germany accelerated. A new East German Chief of State, Egon Krenz, opened the Berlin Wall and promised political changes to try to stem the flow. These developments offered opportunities for German-American cooperation in elaborating a common plan for Central and Eastern Europe, but they also raised risks of German-American disagreement because their intense impact on West German opinion and on *Ostpolitik* could propel the Federal Republic on a separate course if no common policy could be achieved.

But I did not write this book only to list disagreements. I wrote it to analyze the basic trends in relations between the two states and their people. Although I will try to review all the many issues that have surfaced between the two states, I will try at each point to give at least my perception of *why* things have happened as they have, as crises are most treacherous when they are not understood.

General Charles de Gaulle once spoke of the passing of *l'Algérie de Papa.* We are now seeing the passing of *l'Allemagne de Papa,* of *l'Amérique de Papa,* and therefore of *l'Alliance de Papa.* But no American or German could have expected or wanted the relationship to continue as it had been.

As the title of this book suggests, Germans and Americans have become more ready to question each other than before, and both have become uncomfortable with some aspects of their collaboration. But the two countries and their people also remain partners, and even mutually essential partners. That is the basic tension that they need to resolve.

The forces that hold the two countries together are very strong. Many crises have come and gone in German-American relations, and many more have been predicted than have actually occurred. More will come. Not every new one should be seen as a harbinger of some final and irremediable split. But an accumulation cannot be taken lightly, because it may reveal something more fundamental.

It has been said that German-American scholars are either apologists or alarmists. I try to be neither. I do not apologize for either country. I have lived in both, worked in both, and have tried here to be as fair as possible in describing the views and actions of both. As for being alarmist, I do not point with alarm, but I do occasionally point with concern.

I have also tried to be objective in the domestic politics of both countries, especially as I know and respect many persons in Bonn and Washington who grapple with the daily complexities of alliance politics, and my friends are on all sides of the political spectrum. No word or sentence of mine should be interpreted to favor or oppose any party or person in either country. I have not attempted to analyze German-American relations in terms of the domestic politics of either country, as the factors central to my concerns go beyond parties to the objective relationship between the two countries.

If I have a prejudice in writing this book, it is not for either country or for any person but for the importance of what they have done and can do together. Sophie Tucker once wrote that "I've been rich and I've been poor, and believe me rich is better." I could write that "I've experienced German-American friendship and German-American hostility, and believe me friendship is better."

The organization of the book is slightly unusual and deserves explanation. The first chapter is the setting, an analysis of the present and of current problems. The second chapter then goes back to 1945 and contains a brief chronological review since World War II. The review is not meant to tell the full story but only to underline some aspects of the post-1945 evolution that are important for an analysis of where the relationship now stands. There are excellent histories of German-American relations since World War II, which I've cited in the endnotes. This is not the place to duplicate them.

The organization after that chapter is topical, with several chapters on security and one each on *Ostpolitik,* economics, and public opinion. Those chapters analyze current issues on the basis of the setting described in the first chapter and the broad evolution shown in Chapter 2. The conclusion attempts to understand what the new relationship can mean for both countries, what the prospects might be, and some things that can be done.

Describing the many elements of such a close relationship in one slim volume demands compression. Each chapter could be a book; each subtopic could be a chapter. But the object of this work is not to describe every issue in detail. It is to present an evolution and to illuminate principal trends, while attempting to put many superficially separate elements into a coherent whole.

The book is not an historiographical essay. I will not try to resolve the many issues that have been subject to revisionist and counterrevisionist studies. Instead, I have summarized what happened based on principal sources because I had the limited objective of highlighting trends in German-American relations and not of writing a new history of the cold war.

By the same token, scholars may note that I have footnoted many events from both German and U.S. sources but that there are moments when I write about specific incidents or in quite broad terms without such footnotes. Those passages reflect my own knowledge and interpretations, based either on personal experience or on conversations with dozens of German and American officials, scholars, or friends. I have been involved in German-American relations for much of my adult life, in Europe and the United States, and occasionally take the liberty of writing what I have seen or what I have learned directly.

Although I wrote this work on my own initiative because I thought it was now necessary, portions of it were researched separately and earlier under grants or other forms of support from the Center for Strategic and International Studies, the Institute for Foreign Policy Analysis, or the Institute for International Economics. None of these institutions bear any responsibility for the opinions in this book, which are my own, but I want to thank them for their support.

I would also like to express my appreciation to the American Institute for Contemporary German Studies, the Foreign Broadcast Information Service (FBIS), the Friedrich Ebert Stiftung, the Friedrich Naumann Stiftung, and the Konrad Adenauer Stiftung for providing me with miscellaneous materials that I used in the research.

I especially want to express my appreciation to the library at the U.S. Department of State for making many books and newspapers in both languages available, to the German Information Service in New York for the German official *Bulletin* as well as the publications "Statements and Speeches," the "Deutschland-Nachrichten," and "The Week in Germany," to the German *Presse-und Informationsamt* for "Aktuelle Beitraege zur Wirtschafts-und Finanzpolitik," and to the *Bundesbank* for its monthly and annual reports.

Finally, I would like to thank the many American and German friends who became swept up in this work, willingly or unwillingly, as I talked to them about it, and I especially want to thank my family for being infinitely patient and supportive.

W. R. Smyser

1

The Setting

The New Germany

When I wrote my first book on German-American relations almost ten years ago, I observed that the Federal Republic of Germany and the United States were in a position of "equivalence." That equivalence, I wrote, did not constitute full equality, but meant nonetheless that they both bore responsibility for maintaining the international strategic, political, and economic system that protected them and that they had helped to build.

Several of my German friends questioned the term "equivalence." They were uneasy about any word that suggested parity between the United States and the Federal Republic of Germany. They were relieved that I had not written of "equality." One, a good friend for many years, stressed that the Germans had limited ambitions, carefully circumscribed goals, and a distinct wish to avoid giving the impression that they might have achieved, or were even seeking, any kind of international power or influence.

My friends cited the primary American role in defending Western Europe, in maintaining global political and strategic stability, and in managing the global economic system. They saw a much more modest role for West Germany, a role played in the sheltering shadow of the United States, and they insisted that the Germans were satisfied to have precisely such a role and no greater one. They said that German history had shown their country to be better off when it did not assert itself, and that they preferred to keep it this way. They welcomed peace and tranquility, and they did not wish to place either at risk.

As I now turn again to the subject of German-American relations, my German interlocutors are less reticent about the word "equivalence." The same friends who then objected to the word or to the concept now accept it, although they still demur at the notion of equal responsibility. Some of them even accept the idea that there may be broad German-American equality, although with the important reservation that the Federal Republic does not have either nuclear weapons or global security commitments. They feel more comfortable than ten years ago with a greater German role, but they still talk of it in terms of a junior rather than a full partnership.

This modesty departs further and further from reality. From the time ten years ago that the Federal Republic had merely gained some responsibility for global events, it has now arrived at the point where it often has as much capacity as Washington to exercise influence in a number of areas. The Federal Republic's diplomacy with Moscow, its policy in international economic affairs, or its role in the European Community, help set the course for the world as a whole. Its attitudes toward European defense can shape the NATO agenda and determine NATO readiness. The one area where equality does not exist, strategic nuclear power, has become neutralized by the global balance and is often only a muted factor in current events. It must be kept in mind, but it is not now at the center of the world stage.

German modesty may also be disingenuous, at least for some. Many West Germans are quite conscious of their influence and are confident about many aspects of the Federal Republic's new role. West Germany not only has power and authority, but it is often prepared to exercise them with much more independence from the United States than ten years ago. It is also ready to distance itself from the United States and to question and oppose American policies that it regards as wrong. It functions more than before on its own, or in a different framework from the American connection.

This evolution represents an immense achievement. It attests to American readiness to nourish an alliance relationship that tolerates diversity and a higher degree of independence than great powers traditionally allow. It also attests to German readiness to emerge as a more autonomous partner, to put an end to the suspicion that Germans could not manage a truly democratic system, and to make its own contribution to the alliance.

Commentators in the 1960s and 1970s often liked to observe that Germany and Japan were economic giants but political pygmies, a description that was not accurate then and which nobody would dream of using today.

The New Europe and the New World

German-American relations do not exist in a vacuum. They are part of a structure of global affairs and they reflect as well as shape the setting in which they exist. As it shifts, so does the relationship.

The situation in Europe and in the world at large has evolved enormously from the time when the German-American tie was forged after World War II. Moreover, it is continuing to evolve ever further from the early post-war years of the cold war and from the detente period of the 1970s.

In contemplating Europe and the world, one can now look back on the twentieth century almost from the vantage point of the twenty-first. From that vantage, the twentieth century in Europe had two main phases. The first was the great European civil war, which lasted thirty years from 1914 to 1945, drew in two great semi-European powers, and destroyed much of the continent. The second was the absolute division of Europe between East and West. This has lasted for more than forty years, but the division is easing. It may not last into the twenty-first century in its present form, as the tensions and conflicts of this century pass from center stage.

The future European setting, therefore, will in some ways reflect an older setting. It will be reminiscent of the times before the world wars, when Europe was at least partly united as a cosmopolitan, economic, social and cultural entity even as its states remained independent and its peoples fiercely ethnocentric and nationalistic. Europe and the world as a whole were then more fluid than in the cold war. Alliances were less fixed. Global structures were less rigid. Balances shifted as nations adjusted their views and their positions, or as they rose and sank in power and influence.

The sense of a return to pan-European existence stirs the imagination of many Europeans, especially Germans. They see the resumption of travel across the crumbling Iron Curtain. They see the fence between Hungary and Austria removed. They see the new business contracts and the floods of tourists. They see the diplomats jetting back and forth, and the reviving flow of ideas and influence. They see political concepts moving from West to East, as in the past. Industrial goods, commercial credits, investment capital, and entrepreneurs, moved from West to East. From the East came raw materials and, before socialism, agricultural goods and a dynamic culture.

The Germans see the slow knitting together of a torn continental fabric that represented the center of their history and culture. Most of all, they see that they might no longer sit at the perilous edge of one world but in the middle of another one. They see the return of something older, larger, and in some ways better even if very far from perfect.

As one examines the evolution of European and Western history, the two world wars and the cold war appear increasingly as an interruption, an implosion and perhaps an aberration. Now, with European

states recovering and the lines that were drawn in the cold war soft-
ening, the shape of the continent is returning in many ways to an
earlier day.

The similarities between many of the elements of the present and
of past European systems should not obscure or conceal the differences
nor the long way yet to be traveled. Europe before 1945 did not know
nuclear weapons. Even though it was fascinated by progress, it could
not conceive the impact of technical developments on economics, strategy, and the totality of existence, nor could it conceive of the continent
ever having to face the many common problems that it faces today
because of technology. No single European power was then as militarily
dominant as the Soviet Union still is today, and the center of the
continent had not experienced the division that still today marks it in
many ways. Yet the direction of the flow toward a reunited continent
represents a powerful force, and Germans sense it more than others.
Certainly more than Americans.

In a broader sense, the end of the twentieth century is witnessing
the relative decline of the superpowers, as such new stars as Japan,
West Germany, and others begin more and more to assert themselves.
That decline is more pronounced for the Soviet Union, which is suffering
an ideological, an economic, and an imperial crisis. But neither the
United States nor the Soviet Union is as dominant now as it was forty
or even twenty years ago.

The New Security

In the new Europe and the new world, as in the one that preceded
1914, both the term and the concept of "security" can be defined very
differently from the way they were defined during much of the twentieth
century. From the early 1900s well into the 1970s and 1980s, the
concept of security was largely defined in military terms. The term
"security studies" after 1945 came to mean military studies, and the
only security experts were military experts. Such traditional instruments
of international relations as diplomacy or commerce seemed irrelevant.
The dominating experiences of the twentieth century, whether at Ver-
sailles, Munich, Yalta, or Potsdam, had left a clear impression that
diplomacy could not guarantee safety. Moreover, although all states
sought prosperity, few if any perceived it as the decisive instrument of
power during the violent struggles that ravaged first Europe and then
other parts of the globe. What mattered was force, and the ability to
use it quickly, massively, and decisively.

But security is a broader and more fundamental concept than military might. In the new world, nations can seek security in that broader

sense, not only in large standing armies and nuclear forces. They can try to use a combination of instruments to find the formula that best suits their interests, capacities, and responsibilities.

In the world that is now emerging, discussions about security need to weigh three different instruments:

- First, and still foremost if no longer unique, is military strength. Force remains the *ultima ratio* of international relations. Political power, as Mao Zedong wrote, ultimately resides "in the barrel of a gun." But military power is no longer alone in its authority, and there are deepening questions about its effectiveness and about its price, especially when it is neutralized by matching power and ill supported at home.
- Second, and growing in importance, is diplomatic, or political, security. States can now, more than at any time since the nineteenth century, extend their security by diplomatic means. Through the intelligent use of diplomacy, a state can increase its range of friends, reassure potential enemies, and form relationships that can achieve certain objectives without the exercise and perhaps even without the existence of military superiority. As the turbulent cycles of revolution have ebbed, diplomacy has been able to function not only across military lines but even across ideological lines to generate a greater sense of safety. During and after World War II, Prime Minister Neville Chamberlain was derided for having believed that diplomacy could help secure "peace in our time," but today negotiations as a means of helping to assure security are again coming to be accepted. That can be seen not only in the growing extent of East-West arms control talks but in a whole range of negotiations about Afghanistan, Angola, the Middle East, and Southeast Asia.
- The third instrument for achieving security is economic. This concept is also growing in importance. The long period of global peace and prosperity since the 1950s has given greater weight to economic power, especially as it has become increasingly clear that military force will not always prevail and that those who do not have it can often also be safe. States with economic weight can speak with greater authority in a balanced world because they are not threatened with imminent destruction. They can use economic leverage to gain political concessions.

The global environment remains the peace of Damocles, but it is not as terrifying as it once was. Fear of nuclear war has restrained the great powers from attacking each other. It has forced them to find and accept peaceful solutions to crises that might once have erupted into war. There is growing evidence that even non-nuclear conflicts are subsiding and can be solved by diplomacy. This could help to bring about a global era of greater stability and peace. Highly volatile trouble spots remain, whether in the Middle East, Central America, South Africa, or elsewhere. But they are not perceived to be as dangerous, or as likely to trigger a world war, as before.

The world may be entering at least a temporary cycle of international political and military stability unseen since before World War I. If those trends persist, political, diplomatic, and economic instruments become even more important because war can seem more distant and military forces can be reduced.

Europeans see the world in these terms more than Americans. Western Europe has now enjoyed peace longer than any other part of the world. Despite Soviet marches into East Germany, Hungary, and Czechoslovakia, Europe has known a greater peace, and a longer one, than at any time since the age of Charlemagne, even longer than from 1871 to 1914. While invasions, insurrections, and wars ravaged Afghanistan, Africa, Central America, the Middle East, Indochina, and many other areas, West Europeans were free to concentrate on their families, their jobs, their vacation plans, and the slow but sure accumulation of prosperity on a continent that had surely suffered during the first half of the twentieth Century as much as any other in recorded history.

This period of peace and prosperity has been all the more remarkable in that no major problem of the cold war years has been fundamentally resolved. Germany, like its former capital Berlin, remains physically divided and has been forced to yield the eastern territories that had been part of the legacy of the Teutonic Knights for a thousand years. Eastern Europe, despite the first budding of freedom, remains largely under Soviet domination, part of a security glacis that the Russian empire has projected further west than ever in the past. The large standing armies of the North Atlantic Treaty Organization and of the Warsaw Pact remain in place, ever alert, ever formidably equipped, and ever in waiting. Nothing has changed, but everything has changed.

Beyond the shift in the East-West confrontation, and in many ways equally significant, is the emergence of a new European institution of the West, the European Community. This institution has gone well beyond its origins as a customs union and coal/steel community to assume a number of broader economic and political roles. That change has helped mark the re-emergence of Europe to global authority and prominence, and has helped advance the influence of its members.

By the end of 1992, in what some have called the "rediscovery of Europe," the Community is scheduled to become a single market. It already has grown to include twelve countries and to become a potential superpower. In economics, it can help shape the world into trigemony with Japan and the United States. In politics, it has stimulated a new sense of European consciousness. It has no role in military matters, but its membership increasingly matches the European membership of the North Atlantic Treaty Organization.

The New German-American Agenda

The increase in West German economic and political influence has come about at a propitious time, when those very instruments of national power carry far more weight than they did in the immediate post-war years. This coincidence has reinforced the Federal Republic's voice and role in international affairs and especially in Europe. Even if Germany is divided, the Federal Republic is an essential and sought-after partner in virtually all the significant issues and events of our time. It has in many ways taken the place of the former united German state in its political and economic functions for the rest of Europe and even beyond.

With greater German power comes a greater German-American agenda. The two countries have to collaborate on solving problems almost everywhere. They have to work together to achieve world-wide political and economic stability in an age in which the dominant and omnipresent reality is change. If Germany is still a center of struggle, it is also a center of influence. That influence radiates into Eastern Europe, even into the Soviet Union, and throughout the European Community. It affects issues everywhere. It reaches into the major international organizations that try to coordinate global policies and operations.

Even in the new European situation, and in the new world order, some of the agenda remains as before. The contest that divided Europe for centuries, the struggle for Germany, has not ended but merely changed its form. In the postwar years, Josef Stalin and Nikita Khrushchev tried to challenge the West's position in Germany and Berlin by bluster and threat, trying to push the front line of Soviet power forward. Leonid Brezhnev, instead of advancing the line, tried to stabilize and legitimize it. Now, Mikhail Gorbachev is attempting to leap over the line, using diplomacy to separate West Germany from the United States.

The German question has dominated European politics since medieval times. It now includes the traditional struggle for Germany as a territory and a people. It also includes the struggle within Germany for stability and for a form of unity that other Europeans can accept. Finally, it includes the struggle to have German support in the great issues of the planet. These struggles interact, and the players change. But the question remains for all to try to shape to their advantage. Germany remains the prize, and the Federal Republic is still only one of the players, but it is a more important player just as Germany as a whole has become a more important prize.

The United States is an essential partner for West Germany in all aspects of the new agenda, whether in Germany, Europe, or the world. It still plays the principal role in determining global political and economic stability. It has also played a dominating role in Europe during much of the century. Its participation in the European civil war on the British, French, and Russian side effectively decided the outcome of the conflict. In the cold war, it prevented Soviet Stalinist domination of Europe. It retains its interest in European events. It does not have the power that it had. But it cannot be excluded except at great cost to itself and to Europe.

The growth of German power, the relative decline of American, and the emergence of the new Europe and the new world have complicated rather than simplified Bonn-Washington ties. The two capitals must now coordinate their policies much more broadly and more precisely than before, and in many more areas of endeavor. Actions that either one of them might take almost anywhere can have an impact on the interests of the other. Washington must pay much more attention than in the past to what Bonn wishes, while Bonn must pay much more attention to its own management of the global interests that Washington used to preserve on its own.

The most dangerous moments for any relationship come when the interests that created it begin to shift, and when the relationship between the partners themselves must evolve in new directions and to a new plateau. That is where the German-American relationship now stands.

The key to understanding present and future German-American relations lies not only in the new instruments of international security or in the new power balance, but also in an appreciation of the exploding breadth of the relationship. One must be able to see with the mind's eye the hundreds and even thousands of German and American diplomats, military officers, trade negotiators, central bank officials, or senior government figures talking and negotiating with each other almost around the clock on almost every international topic. And actions taken in totally different contexts can weigh either favorably or unfavorably upon each other and upon the relationship as a whole.

The breadth and depth of the German-American dialogue becomes both an asset and a liability. It is an asset because it offers many opportunities for collaboration, a liability because it offers many areas for divergence. A German publication that lists organizations involved in German-American relations gets larger every year and now runs over 150 pages.[1]

An annual review of activities devoted to the maintenance of German-American relations is almost equally heavy.[2] Richard Burt, the former Ambassador to the Federal republic, termed it a "mature partnership."[3] But it is different from other partnerships, in part because of the lingering protection element in the relationship and in part because of the vast breadth and depth of the topics on which the two states must collaborate.

Problems arise, therefore, not because of the direct relationship, which is excellent in many ways. Nor do they arise because German-American collaboration has failed in its purposes. In fact, one of the ironies of current German-American tensions is that they arise at a time when the two allies have recorded their greatest successes in protecting Western Europe and in projecting Western ideas into the East.[4] The problems often arise because of issues outside the direct relationship, but issues that the two countries must handle in common and on which their attitudes and interests do not always coincide.

Even as the arguments seem to multiply, Bonn and Washington remain principal allies. For the United States, the German connection is unique because it lies in the strategic, diplomatic, and economic realms. The Federal Republic occupies the NATO front line in Central Europe. It provides the base for the largest single contingent of U.S. forces outside the continental United States. It plays a crucial role in East-West negotiations. It is also one of the three most important economic powers in then world. No other single country anywhere matches the combination of these roles crucial for the United States.

For the Federal Republic, the American connection is at least equally important and diverse. The United States is committed to deterring an attack on West Germany. Its forces man one third of West Germany's borders. It is the world's strongest economic power, and its currency constitutes a major portion of German reserves. It still remains, forty years after World War II, one of the victorious states holding a trustee obligation for a German peace settlement and for Germany's capital city.

The United States and the Federal Republic have developed an almost symbiotic relationship. They are extraordinarily linked in almost every area of activity. They consult and collaborate almost routinely on thousands of different questions. Neither can do anything that hurts the other without hurting itself, and most of the things that either might do to help itself would also help the other.

Their relationship permeates every area of global activity, whether in military security, diplomacy, East-West relations, or economics. In each of those areas, cooperation between the two states can contribute to global peace, stability, and prosperity. But arguments between them can undo much of what they have achieved.

Notes

1. *Addressbuch der deutsch-amerikanischen Zusammenarbeit,* Third Edition (Bonn: Auswaertiges Amt, 1988).

2. Werner Weidenfeld, *Bruecken ueber den Atlantik 1988* (Bonn: Auswaertiges Amt, 1989).

3. Richard Burt, *Deutschland und Amerika, Partner fuer eine Welt im Wandel* (Herford: Busse Seewald, 1988).

4. Walther Leisler Kiep, speech before the American Council on Germany, Dearborn, Michigan, May 18, 1989.

2

German-American Cooperation
Since 1945

The German has been taught that the national goal of domination must be attained regardless of the depths of treachery, murder and destruction necessary. . . .

We must never forget that the German people support the Nazi principles. . . .

American soldiers must not associate with Germans. Specifically, it is not permissible to shake hands with them. . . . Experience has shown that Germans regard kindness as weakness.[1]

After the War

It was with these instructions that American soldiers in 1945 entered the land of Goethe, Schiller, Kant, Bach, and Wagner, a land from which many of their fathers, mothers, grandparents or earlier relatives had emigrated to America.

The soldiers came to save the United States, Europe, the world at large, and even Germany itself from a scourge that Germany had embraced in one crisis only to see it plunge both Europe and much of the world into an even deeper crisis and horror.

The soldiers' instructions reflected the depths to which Germany had sunk as well as the classic American tendency to divide nations into good and evil. The soldiers who read them shared a grim sense of determination to set things right in Europe once and for all.

Little did those soldiers know that they were only the first wave of a force that would shatter the isolationist tenets of U.S. foreign policy and that would remain many decades, as conquerors, occupiers, protectors, and finally as allies and friends.

If the soldiers did not recognize this, neither did their leaders. The United States did not know what it wanted in Germany and Europe after the war. President Franklin Roosevelt, anxious above all to preserve the war alliance and to sustain military collaboration with the Soviet Union as long as possible, repeatedly declined all entreaties by British Prime Minister Winston Churchill and others to negotiate agreements shaping the postwar world.[2]

U.S. policy makers disagreed about what should be done. A number of American officials, led by Treasury Secretary Henry Morgenthau, Jr., favored de-industrialization and other stern measures to make certain that Germany would never again be a threat. Others, including senior officials of the State and War Departments, believed that Germany should be rebuilt after denazification as part of a new democratic Europe that would offset the growing and despotic power of the Soviet Union. Roosevelt from time to time appeared to side with one or another faction but often changed his mind at the last moment. As a result, Washington frustrated its allies by refusing to agree about the outlines of the postwar world even as the victorious armies were entering Germany from east and west, creating their own realities as they advanced.

One thing on which American leaders did agree was that the allies should not repeat what they saw as the mistakes made after World War I. Thus, the United States insisted on unconditional surrender so that Hitler and the Nazis, rather than a new German democratic government, would bear the full responsibility for defeat and guilt. The United States opposed excessive reparations so that German democracy should not again be doomed by an economic crisis. The United States also favored the creation of a new German regime that would be neither authoritarian nor so finely representative that it could become as paralyzed as Weimar had been.

U.S. leaders believed that American public opinion and the Congress would insist on bringing U.S. forces home as soon as possible. They expected Great Britain to balance Soviet power, with other strong and free states stretching between them, and that this balance would keep Europe at peace. They did not immediately realize that Europe, victor and vanquished, had been exhausted and bled by the war and was now incapable of revival without outside help.

U.S. policy began to take concrete shape during the year after the Nazi collapse. The U.S. government, and particularly President Harry Truman, decided that the negotiations with the Soviet Union in the Council of Ministers would lead nowhere. Truman saw Stalin forcing Eastern and Central Europe into communism and totalitarianism. He began to understand that the continent was in a state of collapse and he saw that Stalinism was crushing democratic forces wherever it reached. He concluded that Europe, and especially Germany, needed U.S. help and at least a temporary U.S. presence.

In a benchmark speech at Stuttgart on September 6, 1946, Secretary of State James Byrnes outlined the U.S. policy. He said that the United States would henceforth work toward the economic revival of all Germany, but would be prepared to concentrate its efforts on the Western occupation zones if it proved impossible to spread them across the entire country. Equally important, in view of the forced merger that had taken place between the German communist and socialist parties in the Soviet Zone, Byrnes said that the United States favored the establishment of a German administration, with the German people being given the primary responsibility, under proper supervision, for running their own affairs. The United States believed that this was the only way to stop communist rule in the Soviet Zone from sweeping across all of Germany.

At the same time, Washington and London proceeded to the establishment of Bizonia, a common economic area consisting of the British and American occupation zones. Those zones included some of the most important economic centers of Germany, such as the industrial heartland in the Ruhr and the commercial and agricultural centers in Southern Germany and Bavaria. Those areas, especially the Ruhr, were among those from which Moscow most actively sought reparations.

With these policies, the United States showed its wish to revive Germany rather than to leave it weak. U.S. leaders still believed that American public opinion would force the United States to withdraw all its forces, as most had already been withdrawn, and that it had to re-establish Europe quickly before then. Washington had also come to realize that there could be no European recovery, prosperity, or balance without Germany, and that Germany would have to be brought back from defeat even as the country still remained under occupation and even as no final decision could be made as to its fate.

The Federal Republic of Germany

By 1948, further decisions had to be made. The victors' Council of Foreign Ministers had reached no agreement on the most disputatious immediate question, German reparations to the Soviet Union, nor on any of the more basic issues regarding the future of Germany. Great Britain had abandoned its support of Greece and Turkey, bringing the United States into the Balkans under the Truman Doctrine of 1947. The United States had launched the Marshall Plan, and the Soviet Union had compelled the countries it occupied in Central Europe to stay out of the plan.

In February 1948 Moscow sponsored a coup that overturned the Czechoslovak government and led to the death of Jan Masaryk, a man widely admired in the West as a patriot and a democrat. Coming after the Soviet suppression of political freedoms in other states east of the Iron Curtain, this move probably did more than any other to damage Moscow and Stalin in Western eyes. Hitler's attacks upon Czechoslovakia and Poland had provoked World War II. Stalin's suppression of that freedom not only poisoned attitudes everywhere about the Soviet Union but further tarnished the very process of the four-power negotiations. The term "Yalta" became a dirty word, symbolic of the folly of attempting to deal with Moscow. Many Americans and Europeans concluded that no equitable agreement could be reached with Stalin about Europe, and that Moscow would subvert and violate such an agreement even if it were reached.

In April 1948 the Soviet Union imposed a blockade on the Western sectors of Berlin in response to a decision by the United States, Great Britain and France to introduce a currency reform in their German occupation zones. After thirteen months of an allied airlift that proved able to supply the city with basic necessities, the blockade was lifted in May 1949. By then, however, the common German-American struggle to overcome the blockade had generated new political and psychological attitudes, reinforcing the links that had started to develop between the United States and Germany.

During the Berlin blockade, American public opinion underwent a sea change, perceiving the German people no longer as instruments but as victims and opponents of tyranny. By the end of the blockade, Americans had also come to believe that only strength and firmness could prevail against Moscow, and that the Germans were America's allies in that cause. West Germans and Berliners, whose sympathies for America were already strong, came to see the United States as their principal and perhaps only meaningful protector against the Stalinist menace. General Lucius Clay, the U.S. commander in Germany during the blockade, became a hero on both sides of the Atlantic.

These new attitudes began to shape American policy and, therefore, the structure of Europe and of Germany. In Europe, the Western allies in April 1949 established the North Atlantic Treaty Organization (NATO) to provide for the defense of Western Europe and also to lay the foundations for a U.S. commitment to that defense. In West Germany, a constituent assembly in May of 1949 produced a Basic Law that would establish a democratic state system for the Federal Republic. By American and German consensus, the democratic and federalist principles that animated the Basic Law were modeled on the U.S. Constitution. In response, Moscow established the German Democratic Republic (GDR). The political division of Germany thus followed its economic division and the lines of the occupation zones.

The combination of East European repression, the Berlin blockade, NATO and the Basic Law cemented the division of Europe and of Germany, creating the foundation for a long-term U.S. presence that few would have regarded as desirable or possible at the end of the war. The wish to keep a part of Germany out of Soviet and communist control drew the United States away from isolation and into Europe, just as it drew West Germany itself to the United States. These factors established the German-American relationship as one of the basic elements of the new European and global order.

German-American collaboration shaped the map of post-war Europe. If the United States had not decided to re-establish a strong Europe, the Federal Republic would not and could not have been established. If the Germans, and particularly the Berliners, had not resisted Moscow, the United States would not have been able or willing to commit itself to a long-term military engagement abroad. But the decisions that led to these historic developments were not based on any coherent or articulated vision of Europe's or Germany's long-range future. They represented an incremental process in which a series of seemingly separate decisions, some on secondary matters, ultimately led to a major turn of events that went well beyond what the authors of the decisions might have originally contemplated.[3] By the same token, developments outside Germany often had a profound impact on the fate of Germany itself.

The Federal Republic in NATO

Distant events again shaped the fate of Germany in June of 1950, when North Korean forces invaded South Korea and quickly overran most of the country except for a small perimeter protected by U.S. forces around the port of Pusan. Although the United States and South Korea recovered and pushed the North Koreans back, the lesson that the United States and West Germany as well as other Europeans drew from Korea was that Moscow and its clients would not hesitate to attack exposed positions by military force. Washington and Bonn looked anxiously at East Germany, where the Soviet Union was recruiting and training paramilitary forces. They feared that Moscow might attack in Germany as they thought it had in Korea, trying to create a united and communist Germany and then driving all the way to the Atlantic.[4]

U.S. forces were not large enough to fight simultaneously in Korea and in Europe. Therefore, Washington and Bonn decided that West Germany had to raise its own forces to defend itself. West German

Chancellor Konrad Adenauer strongly favored this idea, going so far as to suggest it publicly without advance Allied approval. The United States also favored it, as Truman still believed that American public opinion would not keep a major U.S. expeditionary force in Europe. European opinion, especially French, objected at first. The West Europeans did not want to recreate the German army that had only recently conquered and occupied them. In West Germany itself there was strong opposition and even revulsion. The German people did not want an army that might drag them into another war.

French Premier René Pleven offered a possible solution: To establish a West German army that was not under German national command but was integrated into a new European force to be created under a European Defense Community (EDC). The idea paralleled a West European industrial concept, the European Coal and Steel Community (ECSC). But it was considerably more controversial and was only agreed after extensive negotiations culminating in June 1952 with the signature of the EDC Treaty supported by both Washington and Bonn.

Moscow objected sharply to the EDC, and especially to the revival of a German army. It offered a series of proposals for German unification in exchange for German neutrality. But Bonn and Washington were not prepared to accept Moscow's offer unless free elections were held throughout all of Germany, which Moscow in turn rejected. Two years later, the French National Assembly voted down the EDC Treaty, but the concept of German participation within a Western military force had advanced to such a point that Bonn, Washington, and other West Europeans accepted an alternative plan for the direct integration of West German forces into NATO itself without a separate European structure. To relieve West European concerns, it was agreed that the German forces would not be under separate national command but under NATO orders, and that there would be no West German forces outside the NATO structure and the NATO area. The allies also agreed that the West German army would be limited to 500,000. Most important, U.S. forces would remain in Europe, guarding the smaller European states against their fears of German domination and of Soviet aggression.

The Paris and Bonn treaties of October 1954 established the capstone for the Federal Republic's integration into the West. The West German army was to serve under NATO command. The resurgent German coal and steel industries were being integrated into the ECSC. The twin scourges of twentieth century Europe, German military and industrial might, had been tamed and turned to the purpose of helping and protecting rather than devastating their neighbors. Washington and Bonn had both strongly favored the integrating structures. So had the

West German population, which gave Adenauer's coalition government one electoral victory after another. As Adenauer worked closely with U.S. Secretary of State John Foster Dulles, a warm friendship between them paralleled, and enhanced, the close collaboration of their countries. The two friends, and the two allies, worked together more closely than at any time before and perhaps since.

The United States and West Germany had both given up something to achieve these results. Washington had surrendered traditional American isolationism. West Germany had given up German unity.

Bonn and Washington believed, or at least hoped, that German unity could still come about because the attraction of the West and of the Federal Republic would ultimately make it impossible for Moscow to maintain a separate regime in its own occupation zone. Their judgment was based in part on the uprising in East Germany on June 17, 1953, the first popular revolt in any Soviet occupation area after Dulles had announced his "rollback" concept for freeing Eastern Europe from Moscow. It seemed vindicated by the streams of refugees fleeing East Germany for the freedom and prosperity of the West. Washington and Bonn spoke of persons "voting with their feet." To deepen the isolation of the East German regime, Bonn threatened to break relations with any state—other than the four victorious World War II allies—that recognized the GDR.

Through this combination of policies, the United States and the Federal Republic believed they had achieved the best of both worlds. They had established a democratic German state closely linked to the West, helping to ensure both the security and prosperity of Western Europe. They had left German unification open and had made West Germany so attractive that the GDR could not long function as a separate entity. Even if Germany was divided, the most important part of it was free, and they believed or at least professed to believe that the rest would follow. If Germany had given up unity, as America had given up isolation, it had not given it up for all time.

The Berlin Crisis and the Wall

Soviet leader Nikita Khrushchev and GDR leader Walter Ulbricht may have also concluded that the flight of Germans from East to West Germany would undermine the GDR, and that they could not tolerate the attraction that the Western sectors of Berlin exercised from within East Germany. For this reason, and perhaps to resolve the open questions remaining in Germany, Khrushchev in 1958 began to challenge the Western presence in the city. He warned the Western powers that they had to sign a peace treaty for all of Germany within six months and that, if they failed to do so, he would sign a separate agreement with the GDR which would terminate Western occupation rights by making West Berlin as "free city." The United States, France and Great Britain held several meetings with Soviet representatives to defuse the crisis, but by the end of the Eisenhower administration in January 1961 no progress had been made. Nonetheless, the United States had already generated considerable uneasiness in Bonn by suggesting that West and East Germany could both be represented with observer status at an international conference to resolve the problem.[5]

When President John Kennedy came to power, he and his advisers planned to negotiate with Moscow on many Asian, European, and arms control issues. But they were immediately faced with the Berlin crisis. After a tempestuous and fruitless meeting with Khrushchev in June 1961, Kennedy reinforced U.S. forces in Germany to underline his determination not to be bullied. Nonetheless, Khrushchev decided from the meeting that he could press further on Berlin. As Khrushchev's threats persisted, tension rose. East Germans began fleeing in record numbers, at a rate exceeding 10,000 a week.

The United States tried to reach a negotiated agreement with Khrushchev by limiting its demands to what it termed the "essentials," the freedom and viability of the Western sectors of the city as well as allied access to those sectors. The Soviets and East Germans, recognizing that the list of essentials did not include any U.S. or other Western claims to the city as a whole, sealed off the border between East and West Berlin on August 13, 1961, later fortifying their original barbed wire by building the Wall. The Western allies and the Federal Republic protested, but did not try to use force to reopen the crossing points.

West Berlin morale collapsed at the failure of the West, and especially of the United States, to challenge Khrushchev's and Ulbricht's move. The West Berliners saw it as a sign that the United States might not protect them either. To counter this fear, Kennedy sent more U.S. forces to West Berlin and also sent General Clay back to Berlin as his personal representative. Soviet threats and maneuvers against the access routes continued for months, along with challenges to allied travel into East Berlin, but the morale of the West Berlin population slowly revived as it became clear that the United States would defend its rights in West Berlin more strongly than its rights in Berlin as a whole. The threats subsided in late 1961 after a series of confrontations and ended completely after the Cuban missile crisis of October 1962.

U.S. policy, more than that of any other nation, set the tone and measure of the Western reaction to Khrushchev's Berlin challenge. Other countries followed, even when they suggested privately and sometimes publicly that they would have preferred more forceful action. With the United States being the leader of the victorious alliance, and with Berlin being under occupation statute, neither Chancellor Adenauer nor Berlin Governing Mayor Willy Brandt had the power or even perhaps the inclination to question Washington's lead in public. Moreover, Kennedy and Adenauer had very different views of the world. Adenauer wanted the United States to continue to concentrate on Germany and Europe, as Eisenhower and Dulles had done. Kennedy was the first U.S. postwar President to believe that other U.S. global interests were more important than the Western position in Germany and Berlin, especially in his dealings with Moscow. He wanted to stabilize the German situation and to have a basically quiet balance within Europe in order to address problems in the Third World and to negotiate with Moscow on other subjects.

The Berlin crisis, and the construction of the Wall, marked a crucial turning point in German-American relations and policy coordination. Before that crisis, and before the U.S. definition of its "essentials," there might have been some uncertainty about the extent to which the United States would protect its interests in Germany as a whole against Soviet pressures. The Wall showed that the United States was prepared to defend West Germany and West Berlin but not to challenge Soviet rights in East Germany and East Berlin.

Several major West German and West Berlin governing parties, Adenauer's Christian Democratic Union (CDU), Franz Josef Strauss' Christian Social Union (CSU), and Brandt's Social Democratic Party (SPD), were in position to witness and evaluate American policy in the crisis. Senior German leaders across the political spectrum concluded that the United States would be a loyal partner and friend in West German matters but that any actions that Bonn might want to take toward East Germany or within the all-German context would be its own affair. Some Germans were more ready to undertake such actions than others, but over the long run all were prepared to participate. This introduced into German-American relations the first significant split in political responsibility and purpose.

Detente in Germany

After the Berlin crisis, East-West relations in Europe stabilized. The United States was increasingly drawn toward Asia, especially by its deepening involvement in Vietnam, and was less able and willing than in the past to concentrate on the German and Berlin problem. Within a month of becoming President, President Lyndon Johnson told Chancellor Ludwig Erhard in December 1963 that the Federal Republic should take the lead on German reunification and should also try to improve its relations with Eastern Europe.[6] American political attention and energy were no longer centered on European and German matters.

In the Federal Republic, governments were turning over in the transition from Adenauer's long rule to a coalition of the SPD and the Free Democratic Party (FDP), through several elections and a grand coalition. The two transition Chancellors, Erhard and Kurt-Georg Kiesinger, were both pro-American in their outlook. Erhard was even accused of being too sympathetic to Washington.

Two problems dominated German-American discussions during much of the 1960s: the management of security concerns and the attempts to use growing German economic strength to help defray the cost of U.S. forces serving in Europe.

With respect to security matters, NATO had a difficult and drawn-out discussion about giving West Germany a role in nuclear deterrence to compensate for the presumed decline in U.S. nuclear preponderance over the Soviet Union. Fearing that only a European NATO deterrent might be credible, the Kennedy administration proposed a Multilateral Force (MLF) that could deploy nuclear weapons in the European area and would have German participation. Long discussions made clear that Bonn did not want such a role unless other Europeans supported it, and that few did. Johnson withdrew the U.S. proposal. The substitute proposal for creating the NATO Nuclear Planning Group (NPG) gave Germany the voice it needed without arousing the same Western and Eastern concerns as MLF. Despite some disagreements, Washington and Bonn collaborated effectively on the MLF problem as on other NATO matters, such as the 1967 Harmel Report which gave NATO a role in diplomatic as well as military strategy.

German offset payments for the cost of U.S. forces became a much more contentious bilateral problem between Bonn and Washington. In response to repeated American demands for German purchases of U.S. military hardware to offset U.S. military expenditures in Germany, Erhard tried to muster the requisite domestic support. This proved increasingly difficult as the West German economy faced its first downturn since the days of the post-war economic miracle. Bonn did help fund U.S. forces and U.S. currency exchange rates by various means until the 1970s. Erhard also continued to support the United States by not recognizing the Peoples Republic of China. He backed the U.S. invasion of Santo Domingo and the U.S. involvement in Vietnam against skepticism and outright opposition from strong elements in German public opinion. These steps, along with domestic economic problems, helped undercut his popularity.

The Federal Republic during the 1960s improved its relations with Moscow and with Eastern Europe. Even before he retired from office, Adenauer was making overtures to Moscow. His successors continued and accelerated the policy. Erhard sent a "peace note" to the Soviet Union and other states of Central and Eastern Europe, except for the GDR. The United States supported this note, but Moscow remained lukewarm. Two years later, Bonn resumed relations with Yugoslavia, for the first time opening ties with a country that recognized the GDR and was not one of the four victorious allied powers.

When Richard Nixon became President and Willy Brandt became Chancellor in 1969, Bonn and Washington began an intense collaboration in East-West talks. In accordance with the previous German-American agreement giving Bonn the lead in talks about Germany, that collaboration gave much greater prominence than in the past to the Federal Republic. Bonn played the principal role in many of the negotiations regarding Germany and Eastern Europe and was often sought out by the Soviet Union to help solve problems that had arisen in the broad East-West framework.

The detente process included three agendas that were of importance to Washington, with two of those also being of considerable and even principal importance to Bonn.

The first agenda covered questions about Germany and Berlin that had been left open after World War II, and also covered the future German relationship with Moscow and the East European capitals. This agenda produced several agreements: treaties between Bonn and Moscow and between Bonn and Warsaw; a treaty between East and West Germany; and a quadripartite agreement on Berlin by the four occupying powers. Bonn-Washington collaboration passed through normal diplomatic channels and also through complex personal communications links. Even this close collaboration did not prevent mutual disagreements and suspicions between German and U.S. officials. The Americans often feared that the Germans were making their own separate arrangements, and vice versa. Whatever merit these arguments may have had, the accords that were reached and signed between 1970 and 1971 gave both Bonn and Washington much of what they wanted and made a crucial breakthrough on the German problem.

The second common agenda attempted to address future European stability. This agenda culminated in the talks on Mutual and Balanced Force Reductions (MBFR) and in the Conference on Security and Coordination in Europe (CSCE). Bonn and Washington collaborated closely, but the United States had many more reservations than Bonn about the CSCE talks because it feared that those talks would appear to sanction Soviet suppression of democracy in Eastern Europe.

The third agenda, which did not involve but which certainly interested Bonn, covered the whole complex of U.S. negotiations with Moscow on strategic arms limitation and other subjects of bilateral and sometimes multilateral interest. The U.S. opening to China was part of it, as were the Vietnam talks. The United States briefed senior West German officials on these negotiations from time to time. Bonn remained supportive of American policy even if not directly engaged. Brandt and other Germans believed that U.S. readiness to deal with Moscow on non-German questions created an atmosphere that helped make agreements on Germany easier, but they regarded their own negotiations as distinct and important in themselves.

Detente served as a provisional peace treaty for Central Europe, the peace treaty that could not be negotiated or signed in 1945. Like many peace treaties, it was incomplete, leaving some things open for later negotiation or for historical processes to resolve in due course. It drew the borders in Central Europe along the same lines as the postwar occupation zones. But the process of drawing those lines did not make them more impermeable, as Moscow and the GDR wished, but more open. It was important to the Federal Republic for that reason if for no other.

With the detente process, Germany had overcome the total capitulation of 1945. It had helped shape its own settlement and its own future, not as it would have wished in 1945 but as it and others were prepared to accept twenty-five years later. From that point on, Washington and Moscow could no longer make decisions about Germany without German agreement. The Federal Republic had repaired a gap in its authority and gained greater room for maneuver despite the continuing burden that the imperfections of the settlement—mainly the continued division of their country—represented for many Germans.

During that same process, the Federal Republic and the United States had reached a new level in their international coordination. Each had to work closely with the other, to listen to the views of the other, and ultimately to trust the other. It was an equal diplomatic partnership, although with separate responsibilities and separate agendas. Bonn had to become a player because the problems to be solved had to have German participation and responsibility. By the same token, however, the Federal Republic's newly independent stake in East-West relations could not help but open a subject of possible contention in the links between Washington and Bonn.

Global Coordination

After the detente agreements, the center of gravity for German-American relations shifted elsewhere. The subjects that had dominated discussions between Bonn and Washington for the first decades after 1945, especially the future of Germany and Berlin, moved off the center of the agenda by the latter 1970s and the 1980s. This did not mean that they had become irrelevant or negligible. Allied coordinating groups in Bonn and Berlin continued to consult almost daily, as they still do, about the implementation of certain aspects of the detente agreements. But the main burden of political concern moved to other subjects.

The shift in topics did not favor German-American cooperation. It meant that Bonn and Washington increasingly had to consult on topics on which they did not agree as they once had on Germany and Berlin. The 1970s and 1980s illustrated the new reality.

New governments came to power in both Bonn and Washington during the 1970s. In the Federal Republic, Helmut Schmidt became Chancellor. In the United States, several years later, Jimmy Carter became President. The juxtaposition of these two leaders, with their widely divergent attitudes about policy and politics, represented the greatest split between the world views and personalities of the leaders in Washington and Bonn since the founding of the alliance, even greater than the contrast between Kennedy and Adenauer. Both made valiant efforts to work together, but their contrasting perspectives could not help but complicate solution of the increasingly difficult issues that faced the alliance.[7]

From the beginning of Carter's administration, the Federal Republic opposed a number of American policies. It rejected U.S. requests to cancel the sale of German machinery for nuclear reactors to Brazil, although both sides tried to find face-saving formulas. It also rejected U.S. proposals that West Germany provide the "locomotive" to pull the world out of the 1974–1976 recession. Schmidt and Foreign Minister Hans-Dietrich Genscher both disagreed with U.S. tactics to promote Soviet respect for human rights, a matter that was important for American public opinion. They wanted and supported further Soviet-American arms control agreements, but criticized Carter's initial proposals for large reductions in nuclear arsenals. They finally supported SALT II, but the damage to detente collaboration had been done.

Bonn and Washington continued to work closely on a wide range of political, strategic, and economic issues, but the mood of the relationship was often dominated by argument rather than agreement, and by increasingly acerbic relations between the principals.

Despite these differences, the two capitals were able to work together to solve one principal alliance strategic problem, countering the Soviet development and deployment of the SS-20 missiles that threatened Western Europe. Schmidt raised this subject forcefully and publicly during a speech in late 1977. After extensive NATO consultations, in which both Bonn and Washington were heavily involved, a NATO agreement in 1979 provided for stationing of U.S. intermediate-range missiles to counter the Soviet threat and for a parallel negotiating track.

The greatest single problem in the relationship during the latter 1970s was over the development and deployment of the Enhanced Radiation Weapon (ERW), popularly known as the Neutron Bomb. The ERW's military usefulness as a warhead with limited damage radius was far exceeded by the intensity of the political attacks upon it, including the charge that it was "the ultimate capitalist weapon" because it had allegedly been designed to "kill people without destroying property." The problem produced an elaborate German-American minuet. The United States was prepared to initiate production, but only if West Germany would promise in advance to station the warheads on its territory. The German government was prepared to accept stationing, but not to accept German "singularity." Schmidt said that Bonn would agree to stationing only if other continental NATO countries also did so and if it was made clear that U.S. production was not initiated only to supply a German need.

After protracted and painstaking consultations between U.S. and German officials, Schmidt in March 1978 stated that he was ready to support production and deployment on the basis of a formula that eliminated German "singularity" but that still required him to shoulder a heavy domestic burden. He made the decision despite bitter opposition within the SPD. At that point, however, Carter changed his mind, citing moral as well as political reservations about the weapon and stating that his senior advisers had acceded to arrangements that he had not authorized. Carter's decision exacerbated differences between him and Schmidt although these were later somewhat relieved by a Carter visit to Bonn and by successful if belated cooperation on intermediate-range missile deployment.

The arrival of Ronald Reagan and Helmut Kohl in 1981 and 1982 did not so much change the problems confronting German-American relations as their tone.[8] Kohl was strongly pro-American in his personal attitudes, probably more than any Chancellor since Erhard. He shifted German policy closer to that of the United States under its new administration. He and Reagan established a good relationship from their first meeting and remained personally friendly. They were able to work closely together in managing the actual deployment of new U.S. intermediate-range missiles in West Germany in response to the SS-20s. Their mutual confidence undoubtedly helped overcome some of the more thorny problems that surrounded the stationing of the missiles. It also contributed to a positive German-American mood even as many

Germans, especially the press and intellectuals, increasingly criticized Reagan foreign policies and actions in Central America or against Libya.

Reagan visited Germany several times, either for official state visits or for working visits in the context of global consultations. He visited Berlin and called for the Soviet Union and the GDR to tear down the Wall. In May 1985, at Kohl's invitation, he visited the Bitburg German military cemetery, a visit that became highly controversial in the United States when the international press revealed that 48 members of the Nazi elite SS forces were also buried there. Reagan carried out the visit in spite of the controversy, but matched it with a visit to the Bergen-Belsen concentration camp to show that his visit to Bitburg was not intended to honor or exculpate SS policies and actions. To underline his friendship for Kohl, West Germany, and the Germans as a whole, he said at the cemetery that the United States did not believe in the concept of collective guilt.

Before Reagan left office, Kohl visited him again in November 1988 to thank him personally for what he termed the "good years" of cooperation and for what they had accomplished together.[9] He also met with George Bush, then the President-elect, and exchanged mutual reassurances of collaboration.

But Kohl's visit to Washington not only underlined the personal good feeling between the American and West German leaders. It also showed that German-American relations had become so broad and so sensitive that even the best of personal relationships could not overcome all the difficulties. During Kohl's visit, he repeatedly had to defend himself and his government against suspicions that West German policy toward Moscow and East Germany was too accommodating. Reagan and other U.S. officials also used the visit to urge Kohl and members of his delegation to block the sale of German machinery for a chemical plant in Libya that might make poison gas. Those sales, and the entire problem of German exports to potential chemical weapons producers, exploded shortly after Kohl's return to Bonn into a nasty German-American crisis even as both Reagan and Kohl had hoped to end their cooperation on a positive note.

Bush quickly found himself embroiled in another German-American issue within weeks after assuming office, as Bonn pressed hard for early East-West negotiations to reduce the number of short-range nuclear weapons in Europe, weapons that would explode either on West or East German territory if they were ever launched. Although Bush and Kohl were able to ease some of the German-American differences during the 40th anniversary NATO summit in late May 1989, the issue was not fully resolved and continues to disrupt German-American relations and NATO strategy.

Evolution

The review of main elements in German-American collaboration over the past forty-five years shows the evolution to the situation shown in Chapter 1:

1. Rising West German influence, linked with greater capacity to determine its own fate, and often manifest as much in opposition to, as with the encouragement of, the United States. There are moments when it almost seems as if the Federal Republic could gain maturity only by demonstrating its independence from its early protector.
2. A constantly widening agenda, and one that moves progressively from an exclusive concern with Germany and Berlin to a much broader range of issues, but that does not completely abandon those early questions either.
3. As the agenda widens, greater possibilities for tension and disagreement, with part of the tension resulting from the fact that the old questions cannot be completely solved even as new ones multiply.

As the twentieth century draws to an end, the United States still retains some of the mentor and protector functions that it assumed in the middle of the century, and the Federal Republic still needs a certain protection. But they function elsewhere as equal or virtually equal partners. This is a tension that forty-five years of German-American relations have not been able to resolve, and that makes the relationship both essential for the two partners but also harder to manage than any other.

The number of German-American problems, and the sharpening of the discussion, raise an important question: Have American interests and West German interests begun to diverge to the point where the relationship established at the time of West Germany's founding in 1949 can no longer continue? If they have, what does it mean, and what kind of relationship is possible? If they have not, why so many problems all at once?

As the German-American agenda has grown so wide that it can no longer be expected to produce consistent unanimity, it can also no longer be encompassed within a single subject area. The next five chapters will, therefore, present different aspects of the relationship separately, with some extra attention to strategic issues because they are crucial and also generate many problems. After that, the separate strands will again be pulled together for a discussion of public attitudes and an evaluation of how the relationship can be expected to evolve.

Notes

1. Excerpts from "Special Orders for German-American Relations," cited in Heinz Gatzke, *Germany and the United States* (Cambridge, Mass.: Harvard University Press, 1980), pp. 151–152.

2. This discussion of U.S. policy toward Germany, as well as of the situation in Germany during the latter war years and the first postwar accords, is drawn from the following accounts: John H. Backer, *The Decision to divide Germany* (Durham, N.C.: Duke University Press, 1978), pp. 1–60; Gatzke, *Germany and the United States*, pp. 154–178; Wolfram F. Hanrieder, *West German Foreign Policy, 1949-1963* (Stanford: Stanford University Press, 1967), pp. 13–33; Manfred Jonas, *The United States and Germany* (Ithaca, N.Y.: Cornell University Press, 1984), pp. 264–274; Hans Georg Lehmann, *Chronik der Bundesrepublik Deutschland, 1945/49-1983* (Munich: C. H. Beck, 1984), pp. 15–20; Roger Morgan, *The United States and West Germany* (London: Oxford University Press, 1974), pp. 9–27; Henry M. Pachter, *Modern Germany* (Boulder, Colo.: Westview Press, 1978), pp. 269–277. Selected documents are reproduced in U. S. Department of State, *Documents on Germany, 1944-1985* (Washington: U. S. Department of State, 1987), pp. 1–139. The influence of the U.S. Constitution on the Basic Law is described by Kurt Rabl, Christoff Stoll, and Manfred Vasold, in *From the U.S. Constitution to the Basic Law of the Federal Republic of Germany* (Graefelding: Moos, 1988).

3. Backer, *The Decision to divide Germany*, p. 171.

4. Arnulf Baring, *Aussenpolitik in Adenauers Kanzlerdemokratie* (Munich: R. Oldenbourg, 1969), pp. 76–162; *Documents on Germany*, pp. 198–431; Hanrieder, *West German Foreign Policy*, pp. 33–92; Lehmann, *Chronik*, pp. 25–40; Morgan, *The United States and West Germany*, pp. 31–47.

5. McGeorge Bundy, *Danger and Survival* (New York: Random House, 1988), pp. 358–390; U.S. Department of State, *Documents*, pp. 521–830; Gatzke, *Germany and the United States*, pp. 178–192; Jonas, *The United States and Germany*, pp. 297–301; Morgan, *The United States and West Germany*, pp.75–114.

6. A great deal has been written about detente and about the arrangements made between the United States, the Soviet Union, France, Great Britain, West Germany and East Germany during the years from 1969 to 1973. For the summary purposes of this discussion, the principal sources have been Gatzke, *Germany and the United States*, pp. 195–228; Christian Hacke, *Weltmacht wider Willen: Die Aussenpolitik der Bundesrepublik Deutschland* (Stuttgart: Klett-Cotta, 1988), pp. 103–217; William G. Hyland, *Mortal Rivals* (New York: Random House, 1987), pp. 27–35; Henry A. Kissinger, *White House Years* (Boston: Little, Brown and Co., 1979), pp. 821–833; Lehmann, *Chronik*, pp.

90–96; Morgan, *The United States and West Germany,* pp. 119–217. A detailed account of the Johnson-Erhard-Kiesinger period is by George McGhee, *At the Creation of a New Germany* (New Haven, Conn.: Yale University Press, 1989).

7. The discussion of the German-American relationship during the latter 1970s is drawn from many sources, including the author's personal experience, but principal published references were Zbigniew Brzezinski, *Power and Principle* (New York: Farrar, Strauss, Giroux, 1985), pp. 131–132, 301–302, 309–310, and 462–488; Hacke, *Weltmacht wider Willen,* pp. 221–286; Cyrus Vance, *Hard Choices* (New York: Simon and Schuster, 1983), pp. 68–69, 85–86, and 93–98.

8. For a good initial summary of the Reagan-Kohl period, see Hacke, *Weltmacht wider Willen,* pp. 326–357.

9. *New York Times,* November 16, 1988; *Washington Times,* November 16, 1988.

3

Security: NATO and the Division of Labor

Accidents and Their Aftermath

On Sunday, August 23, 1988, over 300,000 Germans gathered at Ramstein U.S. Air Force Base for the annual air show. They came to enjoy a day in the sun and a display of aerial acrobatics by American and other NATO aircraft. A team of Italian flying aces, the Tricolor Arrows, performed a spectacular but difficult maneuver called "an arrow through the heart," in which a single jet pierces through the center of a heart-shaped figure traced by the contrails of his colleagues.

This time, however, the arrow did not fly through the heart but crashed into several other aircraft. The jets exploded above the crowd, hurling debris, shrapnel, and flaming fuel over thousands of spectators. More than 60 persons died. Hundreds were wounded, many of them disfigured for life.

The incident and its aftermath reflected in microcosm many of the problems surrounding the presence in West Germany of one of the greatest concentrations of armed might in the history of the earth: almost a million soldiers, over 15,000 tanks and artillery pieces, 3,000 aircraft and close to 4,000 nuclear warheads; all squeezed into a country no larger than the U.S. state of Oregon along with 60 million German civilians. There the soldiers and airmen must live, train, exercise, drive, shop, and play, often near or in highly populated areas. Almost half of the soldiers and their equipment are not German but represent allied countries, and a quarter million are Americans. Many are in Germany under legal arrangements that were made when the Federal Republic of Germany had barely emerged from devastation and conquest.

Those legal arrangements, however, suddenly became an issue on August 23. The newly appointed German Defense Minister, Rupert Scholz, announced that there would be no more aerial acrobatics in German airspace after the Ramstein incident. He then had to be reminded, by the U.S. Embassy and by some of his own advisers, that decisions about the use of West German airspace were not exclusively his government's to make. Suddenly, a human tragedy had produced a German-American defense issue. The United States, Germany's principal ally, appeared to be threatening instead of protecting Germany's safety and sovereignty.

The legal arrangements for German airspace were not capriciously created to frustrate German autonomy. They were part of a complex of postwar agreements intended to permit the unfettered operations of the NATO forces that were to protect the young and weak German democracy against what was regarded as a likely and perhaps early attack from the East. Many of those forces had to be foreign, especially at the beginning, and the Status of Forces agreements had been carefully and not easily negotiated with the aim of preserving German sovereignty. But a great deal had changed by 1988. For the West German people, who had developed one of the world's most advanced and influential states over a period of forty years, and who were increasingly convinced that the Soviet threat was diminishing, the sudden and forceful reminder of residual allied military rights at a time of mourning only underscored what seemed to many as a pointless anachronism.

Other incidents followed the accident at Ramstein. An American fighter-bomber crashed at the town of Remscheid near Duesseldorf, killing six people and wounding fifty. Plans for stationing a new U.S. helicopter squadron provoked protests in towns adjoining the base. Growing complaints about low-level flights by NATO aircraft reflected West German dissatisfaction with the considerable presence and operations of German and allied forces in their territory. There was growing irritation about the 2,000 NATO maneuvers held on German soil. The German population, long accustomed to the operations of the NATO forces and relatively tolerant toward their presence, had increasingly shifted from acceptance to opposition, and the slowly growing concern hit a boiling point after the air crashes. Allied forces reduced the number of low-level flights and maneuvers, even though they worried about readiness, so as not to generate further irritation.

Given the apparently conciliatory tone emanating from President Gorbachev in Moscow, more and more Germans were asking themselves whether so much readiness was really necessary.[1] And, as so often happens in Germany, the American and West German governments had to be at the center of the problem and of efforts to solve it.

The High Arch

The line that the victorious powers drew after World War II through the center of the German nation, between such ancient states and bishoprics as Hanover, Hessen-Kassel, Brandenburg, Saxony, Wuerzburg and Bayreuth, has become the border between East and West Germany. It is also the strategic boundary between the United States and the Soviet Union and their respective alliances. Most significantly, it is the political boundary between governments based on the democratic principles and traditions of the West and those based on the principles of Marxism as transfigured and implemented by Leninism. It has now stood for almost half a century.

The border between the Germanies is also one of the most important elements of the German-American relationship. It constitutes a crucial point for their security collaboration, the terrain on which their united efforts must provide effectively for their common defense.

Defense cooperation between the United States and the Federal Republic has been and remains the principal link in German-American relations. It is the long high arch of the Atlantic alliance. It has also consistently been one of the most sensitive areas of German-American collaboration. Despite the close friendship between Washington and Bonn, as between many individual German and American military officers, management of defense relations has frequently led to friction. Many of the disputes have drawn in other NATO members. Even within the context of their common strategic interests, Washington and Bonn have often disagreed about military strategy, tactics, organization, hardware, burden-sharing, or security collaboration outside the NATO area. Nonetheless, even the most thorny problems have been solved, and German-American common defense efforts hold the NATO structure together.

West Germany needs allied protection. It is, by superpower standards, a small state, covering only a portion of the former territory of the German empire. But even what remains is some of the most important strategic real estate in the world. It lies at the edge of a Soviet imperium that now covers much of Europe and Asia. If the Soviet Union was inclined to bully, the Federal Republic without strong allies could only protect itself by becoming a virtual garrison state—even beyond the Prussian model—or by persistently placating Moscow. In this sense, the U.S. guarantee protects not only West German territory. It also protects the West German body politic from having to debate and decide some of the hideously cruel choices that might have to be made if the Federal Republic faced Russia alone or with weaker and less committed friends.

The American interest is perhaps less immediately obvious, but it is equally important. West Germany offers the main continental pedestal on which U.S. Atlantic and European power rests. It guarantees that the United States will not have to return to Europe for yet a third time to prevent its domination by a hostile state. It helps to give the

United States solid assurance of a friendly continent on the opposite shore of the Atlantic. It anchors what one German has termed the "Pax Atlantica."[2]

After forty years of the North Atlantic alliance and thirty-five years of German NATO membership, the imperatives that created and shaped the alliance are often forgotten. Yet the strategic reality and the mutual dependency that it creates still remain at the center of German-American relations and of the entire complex of Western deterrence and defense.

Complementarity

The special nature of the German-American strategic link furnishes many of NATO's problems, like many of NATO's strengths. The collaboration is complementary, not supplementary. The main strategic border is in Germany. The main strategic weapons are in the United States. Each country. therefore, has a different perspective and a different role. Each brings something different, just as each needs something different. The differences in their responsibilities and contributions generate problems but ultimately sustain the tie. It is clear to both that neither could do alone what they can do together.

The NATO system is essential to German-American security relations. Although many German-American discussions on strategic, tactical, or arms control questions are bilateral, they deal with matters that concern the alliance as a whole, that must finally be addressed in an alliance context, and that often can only be solved within the alliance framework. Many problems that could not be handled on a purely bilateral basis take on a different form in the multilateral context and in a multilateral discussion. Even though an alliance can be a slow and frustrating forum, its members often find it easier to agree, and to justify that agreement, when the entire coalition is at stake.

Persons who have not participated in the alliance dialogue—or polylogue—may find it difficult to appreciate or even to imagine the personal friendliness, the frankness, and the cooperative spirit in which discussions are usually conducted, even when issues are contentious and views differ strongly. Some of that results from long-standing personal relationships; some from a common sense of purpose. NATO helps bridge many a gap, for German-American as well as other disagreements, partly because others as well as the parties concerned in a dispute have a stake in its successful resolution.

U.S. nuclear and conventional forces serve two main purposes for Germany and the alliance as a whole:

First, they provide deterrence, the threat of massive intervention that protects America's friends, interests, and forces. The U.S. presence means that any state that attacks the NATO area is risking direct, overwhelming, and perhaps immediate retaliation, possibly far from the actual scene of the fighting. The nuclear forces could strike military and other installations on the territory of any Warsaw Pact state. Even if a Warsaw Pact attack were successful on the ground, the attacker could suffer irreparable harm. This is the ultimate instrument available to a superpower, providing unmatched and unmatchable protection, but a protection sometimes feared as much as welcomed.

The U.S. nuclear threat presents the Soviet Union with a most serious dilemma. If Moscow chose to attack Western Europe, it would risk retaliation by U.S. nuclear weapons not only against the attacking forces but also against rear installations and, perhaps, against Soviet territory itself. If the Soviet Union decided to preempt that threat by attacking U.S. nuclear weapons sites, especially with nuclear strikes of its own, it might change the character of the conflict. This would nullify the principal Soviet advantage, which is in conventional forces. It would also expose Russian and East European territory to nuclear attack and to nuclear fall-out.

The nuclear element in the NATO arsenal is particularly significant because the Soviet Union, the only European country that might conceivably attack West Germany, cannot be fully deterred by conventional weapons. Conventional battles on the central front would be fought on German, not Russian, territory, and there would be few if any sites in the Soviet Union that would be valid targets for a conventional attack. That might change over time as more powerful and more precise conventional weapons are developed and deployed, but only very slowly. Therefore, if the Soviet Union is to be militarily deterred it must be with nuclear weapons.

To reinforce their deterrent function, U.S. nuclear weapons in Europe represent the link, or the "coupling," between Western Europe and the U.S. strategic deterrent. Since U.S. nuclear as well as conventional weapons systems are potentially engaged in a European battle, the United States itself is engaged as a nuclear as well as a conventional power, and it might well decide to use its strategic systems as well as weapons located in Europe. The Soviet Union recognizes the link, consistently maintaining that any attack upon its territory by U.S. nuclear weapons, even by those stationed in or around Europe, would constitute a strategic attack entitling the Soviet Union to attack American territory itself. The Soviet Union may state this to discourage recourse to American nuclear weapons in Europe, but must also recognize that it merely underlines how any attack in Europe can escalate to the global level.

Coupling and de-coupling with the global U.S. deterrent have long been major issues in American, German, and NATO planning. Many strategic questions are analyzed primarily on the basis of their putative effect on this, whether in real or psychological terms. The debate about what couples and what de-couples has followed some tortuous and even labyrinthine paths because NATO must not only convince itself that coupling will work but it must also convince the Soviet Union. There has never been a definitive agreement that has fully satisfied all NATO states and there probably never will be. Many analysts have concluded that it is best not to define the rules of engagement for U.S. strategic strikes precisely because the very imprecision of their possible engagement helps to add to their deterrent effect.

A second purpose of U.S. nuclear and conventional forces weapons is to fight if deterrence fails. They are powerful enough to affect and perhaps determine the outcome of potential engagements, even those fought principally by conventional means. In a tactical role, nuclear weapons could be used to attack command, supply, and support centers as well as military installations or points at which Warsaw Pact forces might mass for attack. This affects tactics and even strategy. It also affects rear area dispositions.

The mere presence of NATO tactical nuclear weapons can help prevent a conventional breakthrough across the German border by complicating an attacker's planning and preventing him from using forces most efficiently and effectively. Therefore, nuclear weapons enhance conventional defense even if they are not used, only by being stationed in Europe and particularly by being assigned to NATO ground force commands. And that role could be played by other nuclear weapons than American, or by U.S. weapons carried by German delivery vehicles.

Soviet planners have apparently taken account of NATO's nuclear capacity. The Soviet Union has over the last several years changed its tactical plans, exercising with highly mobile Operational Maneuver Groups (OMGs) that would not require massing and that would probe at different points for an exploitable opening while remaining close enough to NATO forces to prevent allied nuclear strikes. Such tactics would offer more flexibility and fewer targets for nuclear weapons.

With the Federal Republic enjoined from having nuclear weapons of its own, the American connection is essential to West Germany's defense. The Soviets understand that. The Soviet Ambassador in Bonn, Yuliy Kvitsinskiy, once said to the Germans: "You cannot be as strong as we are."[3] U.S. nuclear forces balance Soviet power and help protect West Germany.

The U.S. conventional contribution is also significant. There are more than 300,000 American military personnel in Western Europe, mainly in West Germany. They are supported by U.S. nuclear and conventional equipment either stationed with those troops or reinforcing them, and by sophisticated equipment vital to modern intelligence and battle management. In addition, designated U.S. units located in the United States, including five divisions, are committed to rapid deployment in an emergency. Much of their equipment is already prepositioned on European and often German soil.

The presence and commitment of these American troops underlines the U.S. deterrent and also provides a powerful conventional defensive force, permitting the defense of West Germany without forcing the Federal Republic to exceed the Paris Treaty limitation of 500,000. It provides for the protection of Germany and of the NATO front line without compelling the Federal Republic itself to mount a force large enough to make all its neighbors uneasy. It squares the historical middle European problem: how to protect Germany without threatening its neighbors.

The German defense contribution is fundamentally different from the American. It includes no nuclear weapons, although some German systems can deliver U.S. nuclear weapons if necessary and agreed. It does include, however, almost half a million active military personnel, close to the limit, and more reservists. German forces constitute the main element for the conventional defense of the alliance on the central front. Many soldiers are draftees, whose tour of duty lasts for fifteen months (although there have been proposals and even decisions—later reversed—to raise it to eighteen months). In addition, the Federal Republic provides a preponderance of the alliance's conventional equipment, usually of the highest quality.

The West German population has to date tolerated the physical presence and the training requirements of the many separate NATO forces stationed in Germany. This represents a genuine burden for elements of the population, a burden that can sometimes—as at Ramstein and in other recent accidents—be brought home forcefully and painfully.

German-American complementarity has created a situation of mutual dependency that is perhaps unprecedented in the history of the world. The United States is committed to using the most drastic and perhaps suicidal means to prevent an enemy from conquering West Germany as well as other NATO states. It must constantly reassure the Germans, who are very directly exposed, that it is prepared to risk its own existence for their protection but not to exercise that power in a reckless manner. The Federal Republic is committed to permitting the use on its own soil of weapons of mass destruction that are neither in its own hands nor under its exclusive or direct control. Neither would have made these commitments lightly.

The extreme nature of these commitments and of the mutual dependency creates an important requirement as well as an important effect:

- The requirement is an extraordinary degree of mutual trust. It goes beyond treaties, beyond rhetoric, to a sense in each country that the other will do what must be done in the most extreme emergency, acting out of a selfless perception of mutual needs. All the talk about German-American relations comes down to this confidence, to its preservation, and to mutual awareness of all its implications.
- The effect is almost ceaseless mutual scrutiny, searching for reassurance not only that the agreed commitments are intact on paper but that they are understood, appreciated, and respected, and that neither will abandon or abuse the mutual commitment.

Because of this mutual dependency, each country reacts more sharply to the other's actions or statements than to those of any other ally. That dependency and that sensitivity give German-American relations their particular character, filling them with mutual appreciation but also with a tension that can and does erupt in unpredictable ways.

Extended Deterrence and Flexible Response

NATO strategy on the use of nuclear weapons has evolved over the years. In the early 1950s, U.S. nuclear weapons were the principal and virtually the only instrument for NATO defense. When many West Europeans feared a Soviet invasion after the Berlin blockade and the attack against South Korea, NATO planners called for more than ninety alliance divisions to protect Western Europe. The plans never advanced beyond the paper stage and were quietly shelved when it became clear that they could not be realized except at intolerable political and financial sacrifice. American nuclear forces represented a cheaper and more effective deterrent.

The United States had absolute nuclear superiority and could make a nuclear commitment without any fear that American territory might be at risk. The United States and NATO adopted the strategy of massive retaliation, warning Moscow that any attack on NATO would lead directly and immediately to American destruction of the Soviet Union.[4]

As the Soviet nuclear arsenal and its missile forces grew in the 1950s and 1960s, many Western strategic analysts felt that the threat of massive retaliation could not be credibly sustained and they feared that this would undermine deterrence. NATO, and especially the United States, wanted other options than surrender or global annihilation. The alliance adopted a new strategy, the doctrine of flexible response outlined in NATO document MC-14/3 of 1967. It committed NATO and, more specifically, the United States, to the use of nuclear weapons for selective strikes but not necessarily to an immediate all-out nuclear salvo against the Soviet Union. The weapons were to be fired as warranted by the level of a Soviet attack and/or by the likelihood of Soviet conventional victory, with the option of further selective escalation in case Soviet forces continued to fight and to advance. There might be one nuclear strike, or many, against troops or against Soviet territory.

The West German Defense Ministry characterized this strategy by stating that nuclear weapons were to be used "as soon as necessary and as late as possible."

By the 1970s, the Soviet Union had achieved broad nuclear parity with the United States and had a warhead advantage in the land-based Intercontinental Ballistic Missiles (ICBMs) that theoretically could be used for a first strike. The United States had no means to defend itself against Soviet retaliation if U.S. nuclear weapons were used to defend Western Europe. The American extended deterrence commitment seemed even more suicidal and was increasingly questioned.

Speaking at a conference in Brussels during the fall of 1979, former Secretary of State Kissinger warned that further U.S. assurances to Western Europe were unrealistic and even misleading in the light of the new situation.[5] He asserted that the U.S. pledge was bound to lose credibility and public acceptance, and that frequent and emphatic reiteration would not overcome but actually reinforce its implausibility.

Despite these and other questions about the effectiveness of flexible response and extended deterrence, NATO has not formulated an alternative strategic doctrine, especially as extended deterrence has apparently remained effective. There may well be doubts about U.S. readiness to strike in case Moscow attacks NATO with conventional weapons, but even a small likelihood is regarded as sufficient to preserve the peace. No Soviet attack has taken place, even at times when some thought it might come. More important, in terms of West German and West European politics, no Soviet attack has had to be feared.

Most West German and NATO strategic planners have long preferred to have at least some of the U.S. flexible response weapons stationed in Europe so as to maximize their deterrent effect. They have believed that the presence of these weapons in Europe conveyed the clearest determination and readiness—as well as perhaps the necessity—to use them in case of a European conflict.

Nonetheless, German strategists have always insisted that U.S. nuclear weapons stationed in Europe could not by themselves be perceived as the full deterrent. They regard those weapons as a possible warning to Moscow, an omen of potential nuclear war, but not as the full deterrent. One German strategic analyst warned that "Europe will not be able to live" in the event of U.S. strategic inferiority because the U.S. pledge to defend NATO would lose effectiveness.[6]

Some Germans have questioned whether U.S. nuclear weapons on German soil would really trigger the global deterrent or whether they would be used to conduct a nuclear war in Europe only. Egon Bahr has argued that the presence of U.S. nuclear weapons in Europe actually limited the deterrent because the United States might use only those nuclear forces rather than its strategic assets. He said this showed that Washington intended to confine a nuclear war to Europe. By this logic, the presence of U.S. nuclear forces in Europe would weaken rather than strengthen coupling. But most German and other NATO planners have preferred to have U.S. weapons systems stationed on European soil. This is in part because the weapons have a tactical as well as deterrent purpose, but also because of the widespread impression that the Soviet Union would be more effectively deterred if the weapons were in its path and were assigned to the troops that Soviet forces would engage. It is a psychological as much as an intellectual or military construct, but it is not reassuring to those who fear any use of nuclear weapons at all.

Most American nuclear weapons in Europe are perforce stationed in West Germany, as are most U.S. forces. Their number has been reduced since 1980 from 7,000 to around 4,000. Most of the remaining warheads are designed for delivery by aircraft or artillery. Many of the warheads are not for strategic purposes but for tactical objectives and targets. They could be used to conduct a nuclear conflict as well as to deter it, and that is part of their deterrent value.

To weaken both the credibility and the effectiveness of the U.S. deterrent, Moscow has periodically pressed for a "no-first-use" agreement under which both Moscow and Washington would promise not to be the first to use nuclear weapons. The United States has rejected those demands, with West German support, because they would leave West Germany and NATO exposed to Warsaw Pact conventional superiority. Four German strategic analysts even objected when four private Americans urged the United States and NATO to accept the Soviet "no-first-use" proposal. The Germans wrote that a "no-first-use" pledge would make war more likely, and could thus—paradoxically—increase the chances that nuclear weapons might actually have to be used.[7]

Despite German-American opposition to the "no-first-use" pledge, public opinion in West Germany has increasingly turned against nuclear weapons on German territory. Polls have reflected fear that the mere presence of these weapons might make West Germany a more likely target or arena for nuclear war. Moreover, the growing European (and even Western) aversion to all nuclear phenomena, whether civilian or military, has had an effect in Germany as well as in the United States. The fact that the weapons are not German but foreign, even when the foreigner is an ally, cannot help but add to the apprehensions about their presence.

Conventional Forces

The main West German contribution to NATO lies in the conventional forces of the *Bundeswehr.* Those forces number around 490,000. West Germany makes the largest single national contribution to NATO in combat brigades on the central front. It is also either the largest or next to largest contributor in various types of conventional land armaments.[8] Those German forces now represent a powerful fighting instrument, having overcome the stigma and doubts about military service that infected Germany after World War II.

West German and U.S. forces, along with other NATO troops, defend key points along the NATO central front. The United States defends the Fulda Gap and Northern Bavaria. German forces defend approaches to the Ruhr, to industrial Bavaria, and to the port of Hamburg. Even if some NATO units are thin because designated elements may be stationed well away from the frontier, the presence of all those states along the NATO frontier shows that any attack on the Federal Republic would immediately meet a broad spectrum of NATO forces and would be a war against all of NATO not only in theory but in fact.

The basic objective of the American, German, and other conventional forces on the central front is to hold the line as close as possible to the border. Without those forces, nuclear deterrence could be meaningless. Nuclear warheads could strike the Soviet Union and other Warsaw Pact states but West Germany would have been overrun. Moreover, the existence of a strong conventional defense gives more leeway for the decision on using nuclear weapons. At best, the conventional forces could defend the border for a long time without nuclear weapons. At worst, they offer political decision-makers more time to decide what to do with the nuclear deterrent. A senior German general observed that strong conventional forces "reduce the alliance's dependence on the nuclear threat and provide a greater measure of flexibility for the political decision about escalation."[9]

Conventional forces also have two other purposes: To prevent the Soviet Union from occupying a portion of West German territory in a few days and then posing political conditions for withdrawal, and to give time for designated U.S. forces to come to Europe to help in the defense of Germany and NATO.

One perennial discussion theme since NATO's founding has been the appropriate strength of the alliance's conventional forces on the central front. Scarcely a month goes by without criticism of NATO's numerical and equipment inferiority to the Warsaw Pact, or without some suggestion that NATO come closer to parity. But, even if NATO could increase the level of its conventional forces in Europe enough to counter the Warsaw Pact's numerical superiority, the European members of the alliance—and especially the West Germans—have not wanted it. They want conventional forces strong enough to defend for a time but not so strong that the Soviet Union could count on the war to remain conventional. In the very weakness of the conventional forces lies the specter of the deterrent.

That calculation reflects the fundamental dilemma that is the most particularly German element of NATO strategy. Deterrence, not defense, must be Germany's principal objective. One of the most bitter ironies of Hitler's legacy to the German people is that the next European war, whatever its outcome, could decimate the German nation. Any war in Central Europe, even fought with conventional weapons, would be fought in large part on German soil, East as well as West, and would exact enormous German civilian as well as military casualties. Bonn believes that Soviet planners should never be permitted to think that they could initiate any conflict in Europe and have it confined to Germany or even to Europe. Former German Defense Minister Manfred Woerner listed the two principal German strategic objectives as (1) prevention of war and (2) rapid war termination and damage limitation.[10]

Another German defense priority has been forward defense. The Federal Republic has consistently wanted to engage any invading army as close as possible to the border. The Germans want to prevent enemy forces from carrying any conflict deep into West German territory. The policy reflects not only Germany's desire to avoid war on its soil but also the fact that about a third of the West German population as well as about a quarter of its industrial capacity lie within 100 kilometers of the East German border. Such major cities as Hamburg, Hanover, Kiel, Nuernberg, and Wuerzburg lie within or close to that belt. The German government does not want to abandon these cities without making a major effort to defend them. Moreover, much of the border terrain is easier to defend than some of the areas deeper within West Germany.

The United States has accepted the German strategy of forward defense as a political and strategic necessity and has designed its forces and tactics to support it. Under German influence, and with the improvement in German forces, NATO defense lines have gradually been advanced from their original 1952 position, which ran essentially along the Rhine, to a line just to the west of the border with the GDR.

To help protect its front lines as far to the east as possible, NATO has tried to develop plans and forces for attacks behind Warsaw Pact lines to reduce the effectiveness of an attack. New technologies, including drone aircraft, stealth materials and designs, sophisticated radars and sensors, as well as new wide-area conventional munitions, have made such tactics more promising than in the past. NATO has discussed several plans, including the "Air-Land Battle" concept, designed for deep interdiction strikes against Warsaw Pact reinforcements and supplies more than 100 kilometers to the rear of the battle line, and Follow-On Forces Attack (FOFA) that envisages NATO strikes at shorter distances.[11] European NATO members, including Germany, have preferred the shorter distance operations because they have feared that deep-penetration tactics could be misinterpreted, especially since Moscow could mistakenly believe that the deep attacks were nuclear.[12]

These proposals and concepts also involve German-American cooperation. Many of the advanced technologies needed to implement such tactics are developed in the United States. Nonetheless, it is the Federal Republic that must principally determine the balance between its interest in forward defense and its concern about appearing to plan attacks against its neighbors. As the Soviet threat appears to have eased, the latter consideration has become more important even if not decisive.

German-American Burden-Sharing in NATO

The apparent relaxation of the Soviet threat has rekindled in particularly virulent form a periodic NATO and German-American debate about whether one or another partner is doing too much or too little. As the West German population has intensified its complaints about the presence of nuclear weapons and about NATO maneuvers and low-level flights, the United States has had a debate of its own about whether the Americans are sacrificing too much.

This argument is an inevitable result of complementarity. If two partners make different contributions it is difficult to set a common standard of measure for each contribution. It is easy for each country to believe that it contributes something essential to the security relation but that its contribution is unappreciated and not matched by the other.

Many members of the U.S. Congress, whether Democrats or Republicans, hawks or doves, have complained that the United States bears more than its proper share of the costs. From Senators Sam Nunn or Ted Stevens, from Representatives Doug Bereuter or Pat Schroeder, the message is essentially the same: Europe must pay more of the cost of its own defense or the United States will be forced to withdraw troops to reduce its budget deficit. The U.S. Senate has threatened to place a limit of zero growth on the budget for U.S. forces serving abroad. In early 1989, a number of Members of Congress proposed reductions of U.S. forces by 25,000 in order to save money.[13] Even though the U.S. military budget grew rapidly during the early Reagan years, it has recently been shrinking in real terms and the weakening dollar has raised the cost of stationing troops outside the United States.

The obvious prosperity of America's allies, especially the Germans and Japanese, has also made many Americans wonder whether the United States should continue to contribute a much higher percentage of its gross national product to defense than many others (about $1,185 per capita as against $578 in Germany, $697 in Norway, $646 in France, $614 in Great Britain, and under $200 in Japan).[14] Statistics show that the United States spends 6.1 per cent of its gross domestic product on defense, and West Germany only 3 per cent. On the other hand, they also show that West Germany spends as much as France and Great Britain, about $35 billion.[15] Statistical comparisons are, of course, simplistic and misleading. But the statistics can easily generate mutual misunderstanding.

Contributing to the bitterness of the U.S. debate is an American budget process which distorts and magnifies the cost of the U.S. contribution to NATO. Many U.S. forces designated to serve in Europe on a contingency basis are actually stationed in the United States. But the costs of those forces and of their bases, equipment, supporting troops and supplies are attributed to NATO defense, to the point where NATO defense constitutes almost one-half the U.S. defense budget. Yet the actual costs of U.S. forces deployed in the NATO area, while difficult to calculate precisely, are much less than that amount. Much of the debate in the United States is about a phantom figure that vastly exaggerates the actual costs of the forces which the United States keeps in Europe. Nonetheless, if the debate leads to a reduction of U.S. forces in Europe, it will remove precisely those forces that are actually on the line but preserve those held on a contingency basis.

U.S. secretaries of defense have repeatedly testified to the Congress that allied contributions are proportional to their obligations. Secretary Caspar Weinberger reported in 1987 that "our allies continue to make a very substantial contribution to the common defense—considerably more than they are often given credit for."[16] Secretary Frank Carlucci made a similar statement a year later and said that the United States did not maintain its alliances as a favor to the allies but for its own security.[17] He denounced threats to withdraw U.S. forces as a "high-stakes game of chicken." Nonetheless, both secretaries were also urging NATO allies to increase their defense contributions so as to have more burden-sharing.

The West German government has argued that it is second to none in its contribution to the defense of the West. Other NATO states also feel proud of their contribution. A 1988 Eurogroup study insisted that European NATO members were carrying their full share of the burden, indicating *inter alia* that European NATO members contributed 95 per cent of NATO divisions, 90 per cent of its manpower, 90 per cent of its artillery, and 80 per cent of its tanks and combat aircraft.[18] (The Eurogroup study counted only forces actually in Europe, not those on stand-by in the United States.) It also pointed out that the European members of NATO had increased their total defense spending by 34 per cent from 1970 to 1987 whereas the United States had only increased its own by 15 per cent. This is an artificial comparison because it ignores prepositioned U.S. equipment and because the United States in 1970 was engaged in the Vietnam conflict and its defense budget was, therefore, higher than it would have been in peacetime, But it does show that many European NATO states—including West Germany—have increased their defense expenditures more consistently than the United States over the past two decades. Most of all, it shows that Europeans and Americans can both use the complex statistics of burden sharing to support whatever arguments they might wish to make.

The West German Defense Ministry published a study presenting detailed arguments about the level of the German contribution. The study stressed Germany's steady rise in defense expenditures and also pointed to the burden that the German people were carrying in terms of NATO maneuvers, training, and military overflights.[19]

Some Germans, including members of the opposition and journalists, also argued that there had to be a measure that took account of "risk sharing," since the Federal Republic was more exposed to Soviet attack than any other state.[20] The German government has also argued that it is providing direct and substantial help for the defense efforts of other NATO states, especially Turkey and some other southern NATO members, and that this should not be disregarded in the burden sharing discussion.

German popular concerns about their particular burdens, especially due to the presence and activities of NATO forces, has brought about some changes in allied practices. The number of low-altitude flights has been reduced, and the *Bundestag* has debated financing of devices that would simulate low-altitude flying although the simulators would cost over DM 100 million. There were also reports, however, that senior German political figures were very disturbed to hear that American generals had detonated two "tactical missile nuclear warheads" over Central Europe during a NATO training exercise in early 1989.[21]

In NATO, there can be no victor or victory in a dispute about burden-sharing. There can be no commonly accepted standard of value for any national contribution because there are hundreds of possible ways to measure and many more arguments about relative effort and relative sacrifice. But the spread of the dispute under budgetary pressures—especially in Germany and the United States—shows that it can be a very divisive factor in the next several years and could become vicious during any economic downturn.

Coordination Outside NATO:
Libya and Beyond

Another facet of growing importance in German-American relations lies in what NATO has termed "out-of-area" collaboration. NATO's assigned purpose is to defend the Atlantic area, but incidents outside the NATO area itself can have an impact on NATO security. Not all NATO members agree of what could constitute such a threat, nor can they agree on the steps that NATO should take in such a case either as an alliance or through cooperation of NATO members outside the framework of the alliance itself. Such disagreements have been arising with increasing frequency between the United States and the Federal Republic.

This issue reflects as much as any other the problems created by the growing overlap of American and German global interests. The United States, because of its long-standing world-wide presence, is more likely to ask for policy support than any other Western country. The Federal Republic, however, because of its rapidly expanding international role, is ever more likely to have an interest as well, and not necessarily an identical one. This problem led to an acute German-

American crisis in late 1988 and early 1989 over German sales to Libya of equipment that could manufacture poison gas.[22]

Evidence had begun to accumulate in 1987 and 1988 that German companies were selling machinery that could manufacture poison gas for a pharmaceutical plant at Rabta in Libya. The United States was deeply concerned and passed some of the intelligence information to Bonn, at least in part through the Foreign Ministry. The Federal Republic took no action to stop the sales, leaving U.S. officials highly disturbed. Such a plant might not violate international law since production of chemical weapons is not prohibited, but U.S. officials feared that Libyan leader Muammar Kaddafi would use chemical weapons for terrorist and perhaps anti-Israeli operations. Moreover, the sales seemed in direct contradiction to Genscher's own strongly advocated policy to abolish all chemical weapons.

Reagan raised the issue with Kohl during their meeting on November 15, 1988. Kohl did not reveal, and may not have even known, that West German intelligence services had received similar information. When no German action followed soon after Kohl's return to Bonn, the information about the Libyan plant and suspected German involvement was leaked to the American press by frustrated U.S. officials. One American columnist wrote of "Auschwitz-in-the-Sand," asserting that the Germans were prepared to let Libya make poison gas for use against Jews in Israel, as the Nazis had used gas to kill Jews in concentration camps during World War II.[23]

This charge touched a raw nerve. The German government reacted furiously and defensively, arguing that it had received no really convincing evidence of actions by German firms and complaining that the United States was exerting unjustifiable public pressure. A German political leader, Volker Ruehe, stated that the Americans were skating on thin ice by risking German-American relations over this issue and that "the ice has become thinner than many think."[24] Some Germans suspected that U.S. officials were not only behind the leaks but also behind the more aggressive press attacks, although another columnist wrote that Germany should get the benefit of the doubt because of its atonement and reparations since World War II.[25] Kohl called U.S. Ambassador Richard Burt to voice his displeasure.

After further consultations between the two governments, and after further exchanges of evidence, the German government began to review its position. In the meantime, German magazines and newspapers reported extensively not only on sales by one particularly suspect firm, Imhausen-Chemie, but by other companies as well. They traced how German exporters circumvented export regulations through front companies, false documentation, indirect trading routes, and the like. German and American newspapers charged that there were German companies involved in other illegal or questionable exports, such as nuclear materials and missile technology.

The German Government finally revealed that it had obtained earlier evidence about the Imhausen Libyan connection as well as about other companies involved, and that German intelligence as early as 1987 had reported the probability that Libya was attempting to produce chemical weapons. It argued that the information had not been solid enough to stand up under legal scrutiny, but there were also indications that the information was not properly handled in the German bureaucracy.

The opposition parties denounced the government's failure to act quickly as well as Kohl's initial refusal to reveal the full information available to the government. The government told the *Bundestag* that it would introduce legislative measures to tighten export regulations and procedures, as it did.[26] The subject became a major issue for the opposition against Kohl and Genscher.

Once the leaks had taken place and the German debate had begun, the U.S. government tried to prevent the incident from becoming a major issue between the two countries at the beginning of the Bush administration. Washington focused its formal criticism on Libya rather than on the Federal Republic, although some U.S. officials privately voiced impatience and irritation. There was an obvious American sigh of relief when Kohl and other Bonn officials began to detail the entire story. Bush made a point of indicating that there had never been any doubt regarding German objections to the use of German-made equipment for the manufacture of poison gas.

U.S. congressmen did not feel as charitable or as inhibited as the administration, and Senator John S. McCain III severely criticized the Federal Republic during a visit to Munich in January 1989. He stated that he was speaking for many other congressmen than himself.[27] The incident clearly illustrated the need for better German-American as well as intra-German coordination as the Federal Republic's global role grew ever larger.

The chemical weapons question was not the first German-American misunderstanding regarding Libya. An incident in 1986 almost precipitated a crisis of confidence when most European NATO members, including West Germany, refused to support U.S. attacks against Libya after Washington had what it then regarded as solid evidence that Libya had directed a terrorist attack which had killed an American citizen. The reluctance of the NATO allies (except for Great Britain) sparked considerable bitterness in the United States.

The American accusation later turned out to be inaccurate, since Syria rather than Libya may have been behind the attack. That incident, and its outcome, undoubtedly increased European skepticism regarding U.S. accusations against Libya, with many Europeans believing that Reagan felt a particular and even intensely personal hostility toward Kaddafi. But the United States continued to insist that international terrorism represented a threat to the entire Western world and warranted prompt and powerful retaliation if it was to be effectively stopped.

European countries were also slow to support the United States in 1987–1988 when Washington decided to send the U.S. Navy into the Persian Gulf to escort petroleum tankers after Kuwait asked for such protection. European countries, including the Federal Republic, did not initially send ships to help U.S. vessels patrol the Gulf. The United States felt particularly frustrated because the oil being escorted was mainly destined for European and Japanese rather than American consumption.

German officials said that the Federal Republic could not take action outside the NATO area because of limitations written into the Basic Law. After some delay, however, Bonn sent three warships to the Mediterranean to relieve other NATO vessels that could be sent to the Gulf. Great Britain, Italy, France, Belgium and the Netherlands did send ships to the Gulf itself. The German government stated that this decision was made as a gesture of solidarity with the United States, although Washington had hoped for further support such as funds for the operation or vessels actually in the Gulf. Bonn reportedly wanted to maintain good relations with Iran to avoid jeopardizing a German citizen held in Beirut by pro-Iranian kidnappers, an argument that Washington questioned because there were many more American than German hostages.[28]

Americans could not help but notice that West Germany in early 1989 joined other European states in reprisals against Teheran at British request after the Iranian government had offered a reward for the murder of an English author, Salman Rushdie, who had written a book defamatory of Moslems. Bonn seemed more ready to respond to European than American requests for support.

Six months after the incident regarding German sales to Libya, a similar incident arose when the United Sates received evidence of German sales of chemicals for making poison gas to Iran. Secretary of State James Baker reported this to Foreign Minister Genscher during a Genscher visit to Washington. In this instance, however, the German government acted with speed and resolution. West German police raided the company that was to export the gas and the government was able to block most of the shipment. The German government said that the exports had been illegally made, without proper license, and that the new legislation passed after the Rabta incident would help prosecute the company making the illegal sale. Nonetheless, some German officials complained that U.S.officials had again been prepared to leak the information about the U.S. complaint before the Federal Republic really had time to act.[29]

These incidents reflect recurrent differences between the United States and its NATO allies about problems outside the NATO area. Americans resent the differences because they believed that when they undertook to help re-establish the strength and prosperity of Western Europe after World War II they would afterward find support from like-minded countries for problems elsewhere. Most of the time, Europeans meet those expectations. The European states are often America's most loyal collaborators in global enterprises, even if they may differ on the details of how to handle one or another problem. But they do not always agree with Washington's views, especially in places like Central America or the Middle East.

It was not easy for Washington or for American public opinion to recognize that it could not expect European states to be totally in agreement with all its policies. By the same token, the Europeans found it difficult to appreciate the intensity of U.S. official and public irritation.

NATO at Forty

NATO and the trans-Atlantic link represent the fundamental elements that have joined German-American strategic relations for the last forty years. Without them, neither the United States nor the Federal Republic could have the sense of security that they both enjoy today.

But the incidents reviewed in this chapter show that the alliance faces many questions, and that certain aspects of German-American collaboration create problems for each nation's body politic. The security tie may remain as crucial as ever, but many questions are being raised both in Germany and the United States about the way it functions and about whether it can adjust to the new international environment.

Beyond these problems, however, and much more troubling, lies the question of mutual confidence which is fundamental to the complementarity of the security tie, and thus to the entire strategy on which NATO is based. That strategy was first shaped forty years ago and has remained essentially in place, despite alterations made to compensate for shifts in the global strategic situation and despite periodic warnings that it could no longer work.

During the 1980s, both the United States and the Federal Republic have taken actions that appeared to put in question not only the functioning of the strategy but even the concepts on which it is based. These actions, especially when they are improperly coordinated, risk shaking the foundations on which the transatlantic arch has stood. The next two chapters will address those problems.

Notes

1. *Washington Post,* January 2, 1989.

2. Michael Stuermer, "Abschreckung nach Maass," *Frankfurter Allgemeine,* March 21, 1988, 11.

3. *Der Spiegel,* May 7, 1987, p. 118.

4. This discussion of NATO strategy draws heavily upon Leon Sloss, "The Roles of Strategic and Theatre Nuclear Forces in NATO Strategy: Part II," *Power and Policy: Doctrine, the Alliance and Arms Control* (London: International Institute for Strategic Studies, 1986), pp. 57–72.

5. Henry A. Kissinger, "Strategy and the Atlantic Alliance," *Survival,* September/October, 1982, p. 195.

6. Hans Ruehle, "A European Perspective", *U.S. Strategic-Nuclear Policy and Ballistic Missile Defense* (Cambridge, Mass.: Institute for Foreign Policy Analysis, 1986), p. 47.

7. Karl Kaiser, Georg Leber, Alois Mertes, Franz-Josef Schulze, "Nuclear Weapons and the Preservation of Peace: A German Response," *Foreign Affairs,* Summer, 1987, pp. 1157–1180.

8. For a summary of NATO statistics and deployments, see Laurence Martin, *NATO and the Defense of the West* (New York: Holt, Rinehart and Winston, 1985), pp. 18–36.

9. General Wolfgang Altenburg, "Militaerstrategische Ueberlegungen zur Sicherheit Mitteleuropas," Hartmut Buehl, ed., *Strategiediskussion* (Bonn: Verlag E.S. Mittler & Sohn, Gmbh, 1987), p. 387.

10. Manfred Woerner, "Strategie im Wandel," Buehl, *Strategiediskussion,* p. 371.

11. For a summary description, see Jonathan Dean, *Watershed in Europe* (Lexington, Mass.: D.C. Heath, 1987), pp. 63–64.

12. For background on these issues, see: David M. Abshire, *New Technology and Intra-Alliance Relationships: New Strengths, New Strains* (London: International Institute for Strategic Studies, 1985); Yves Boyer, "Strategic Implications of the New Technologies for Conventional Weapons and the European Battlefield," Catherine Kelleher and Gale Mattox, eds., *Evolving European Defense Policies* (Lexington, Mass.: D.C. Heath, 1987), p. 121; *Neue Zuercher Zeitung,* May 28/29, 1988.

13. *Washington Post,* February 25, 1989.

14. *The Economist,* August 6, 1988, p. 15.

15. U.K. Secretary of State for Defence, *Statement on the Defence Estimates, 1989* (London: Her Majesty's Stationery Office, 1989), Figure 7.

16. Caspar Weinberger, *Report on Allied Contributions to the Common Defense* (Washington: U.S. Department of Defense, 1987).

17. *Washington Times,* May 6, 1988.

18. Eurogroup, *Western Defense: The European Role in NATO* (Brussels: Eurogroup, 1988), p. 10.

19. *The German Contribution to the Common Defense* (Bonn: Federal Ministry of Defense, 1986), pp. 16–23.

20. *Wilson Center Reports,* January, 1989, p. 2.

21. *Frankfurter Allgemeine,* June 21, 1989; *Wirtschaftswoche,* May 26, 1989, p. 15.

22. Summary reports of the German-American dispute over the Rabta plant are in *The Economist,* January 21, 1989, pp. 21–22; *Newsweek,* January 23, 1989, p. 32; and *Time,* January 23, 1989, pp. 30–31.

23. *New York Times,* January 2, 1989.

24. *Washington Post,* January 8, 1989.

25. *Washington Post,* January 10, 1989.

26. Presse- und Informationsdienst der Bundesregierung, "Bericht der Bundesregierung an den Deutschen Bundestag entsprechend seiner Entscheidung vom 18.1.1989"; *Financial Times,* February 15, 1989.

27. *Washington Post,* January 29, 1989.

28. *New York Times,* August 5 and October 8, 1987.

29. *New York Times,* June 27, 1989.

4

West German Questions About Deterrence

If U.S. confidence in German policy had wavered at several points during the 1980s, West German confidence in U.S. policy had also been shaken. The United States took several steps in which German officials and strategic analysts saw threats to the foundations of German-American strategic collaboration. American actions and statements challenged concepts that Bonn saw as fundamental to extended deterrence and to the weapons that sustained it. They also raised questions about U.S. policy in a European conflict.

The questions arose largely because of American policies and statements in three areas, the Strategic Defense Initiative (SDI), American-Soviet talks about nuclear weapons reductions, and a new U.S. concept of "discriminate deterrence." Even though each of the questions was answered, the combination left a legacy of confusion and uncertainty in Germany. It helped to tarnish the German-American strategic dialogue. If the U.S. government feared that some German policies had raised doubts about NATO coordination outside Europe, the German government feared that the U.S. policies raised doubts about collaboration within the NATO area itself. In response, Bonn began giving much greater attention to European options that it might otherwise not have considered so seriously. These German measures in turn sparked more U.S. concern.

The Strategic Defense Initiative

President Reagan launched the Strategic Defense Initiative because he and other American military and political figures increasingly questioned whether Moscow was adhering to the strategic regime negotiated into the Anti-Ballistic Missile (ABM) Treaty signed in 1972. That regime, according to the United States, was based on mutual assured destruction (MAD). Under its principles, Washington and Moscow were not to deploy nation-wide missile defense systems against each other, but would rely on the capacity to retaliate with crushing force against any nuclear attack launched by the other.

The MAD regime depended on two conditions: First, that neither the United States nor the Soviet Union would deploy defensive systems beyond the level agreed in the ABM Treaty. Second, that neither would deploy offensive systems powerful enough to conduct a devastating attack against the other and still have enough weapons and defense in reserve to forestall a retaliatory strike. As the U,S. delegation stated at the time, the United States counted on an early Soviet-American agreement for further limitation and even reduction of offensive systems to make the second condition effective.

U.S. expectations surrounding the ABM Treaty were not to be met. The Soviet Union accelerated construction of offensive missiles and placed large numbers of independently targeted reentry vehicles (MIRVs) on such heavy missiles as the SS-18 and SS-19. Although the United States had originated MIRV technology, it did not deploy as many warheads as the Soviet Union.

There was also increasing reason to wonder whether Moscow had ever accepted the MAD regime at all. The Soviet Union began building a chain of phased-array radars around most of its own periphery. In open violation of the ABM Treaty, it built one such radar at Krasnoyarsk in southern Siberia, far from the perimeter where the treaty permitted such radars. It also built massive facilities for civil defense. It developed several types of mobile hyper-acceleration missile and aircraft interceptors.

The combination of these steps led Washington to conclude that Moscow had either chosen to continue a missile defense program despite the ABM Treaty or at the very least had decided to be more ready to contemplate a nuclear missile exchange than the United States. Combined with Moscow's offensive build-up, those Soviet actions generated considerable anxiety about the survivability of a credible U.S. deterrent, a prospect that also had to be of concern to the governments of NATO Europe—and especially West Germany—which relied on the American deterrent. Strategic experts spoke of a "window of vulnerability."

Simultaneously, the concept of nuclear deterrence through mutual assured destruction came under severe challenge in the West itself. Anti-nuclear demonstrators paraded in the United States and Western Europe. American Catholic Bishops denounced all nuclear weapons. An international alarm arose over a highly publicized phenomenon called "nuclear winter," a global freeze that might allegedly result when dust clouds from numerous nuclear explosions prevented the warming rays of the sun from reaching the surface of the earth. If "nuclear winter" could really happen, nuclear retaliation and MAD represented not assured destruction but assured suicide.

Against this background of questions about the strategic regime, Reagan for several years received very encouraging briefings about technical prospects for an anti-missile defense that could intercept the heavy Soviet multiple-warhead missiles in space before they could cast off their warheads on individual trajectories. The space-based defensive systems were to be part of a broad shield of sensors and interceptors that would prevent Soviet nuclear warheads from striking U.S. territory. On March 23, 1983, Reagan announced the Strategic Defense Initiative (SDI), a research program to explore the possibilities for a strategic defense based on the emerging technologies. He justified it with the hope that it would lead to the total elimination of nuclear weapons by making them "impotent and obsolete." Reagan said that he expected SDI to protect U.S. allies as well.

The West German government did not immediately react to Reagan's announcement. It remained virtually silent for over a year, in part because it was already involved in the vicious domestic debate regarding INF stationing and because the doctrine behind SDI was radically different from that which justified the deployment of the INF missiles: SDI as originally presented offered an entirely new concept, strategic defense, not NATO's long-standing and accepted concept of deterrence by threat of retaliation.[1]

Many Germans feared that strategic defense would not protect Europe but would establish unequal zones of security. They saw it as only the first step in the development of Soviet-American missile defenses that would make a European conventional or even nuclear war conceivable by eliminating extended deterrence. Some, especially in the opposition parties, also accepted the Soviet argument that a space-based strategic defense system might be used for offense against the Soviet Union.[2]

When the Federal Republic first took an official position on SDI, therefore, it was cautious and even skeptical. Defense Minister Manfred Woerner expressed reservations at the April 1984 Nuclear Planning Group meeting at which Weinberger formally presented SDI to the alliance.[3] He then gave a press interview in which he observed that deployment of strategic defense would be costly and that defense systems in space could make conventional war conceivable, whereas the system of deterrence based on flexible response had proven to be stable.[4]

In the same interview, however, Woerner said there could be no opposition to an American *research* effort on strategic defense and that the time needed for such research would in itself insure that no system could be deployed for some years. He stated that some response needed to be made to the Soviet effort to create an anti-missile system, but he recommended that this should at first be attempted through negotiations. He also said that the Federal Republic and other allies should be consulted and not just informed on such matters as strategic defense deployment.

Whereas Woerner questioned the strategic aspects of SDI, Bonn's Foreign Office feared its diplomatic implications. German diplomats believed that SDI could lead to a violation of the ABM Treaty, which Genscher had labeled the "Magna Charta" of detente. Bonn saw the detente agreements of the early 1970s, including the ABM Treaty, as a political structure that established East-West relations on a new basis of greater mutual confidence, and the Germans did not want to jeopardize that structure.

It became increasingly clear during 1984 and 1985 that the U.S. government hoped for West German support for SDI. The Department of Defense, in particular, pressed the Federal Republic to express a favorable opinion. In response, Chancellor Kohl established an interministerial group to recommend a German position.[5] He also sought close consultations with the United States, and he put the consultations into the hands of Horst Teltschik, one of the Chancellor's most trusted long-term associates. This appointment also meant that the matter would be handled in the Chancellor's immediate office, not in either the Foreign or the Defense Ministry.

The Soviet Union also began to realize that alliance attitudes could play an important role on SDI matters. Soviet officials in Moscow and Bonn warned the Federal Republic in very serious terms, privately and publicly, about what Moscow described as the dangers of collaborating on the SDI project.[6]

An initial German government statement in 1984 showed a markedly stronger West German interest in the potential arms control implications of SDI than in its potential strategic significance. It voiced reservations about any modification of NATO strategy. It reiterated that the Federal Republic supported SDI as a research program and welcomed alliance consultations, but called for new Soviet-American accords reinforcing nuclear stability.[7]

Kohl's personal statement accompanying the declaration was much broader and more positive but not wholly free of reservations. Kohl expressed his understanding for Reagan's strategic objective, but reiterated the German government's desire to maintain a positive East-West environment.[8] Kohl and his government clearly did not want SDI to provoke an East-West confrontation.

Kohl's statement contained points that opened the door for some significant departures from traditional NATO strategy through the use of defensive systems, but he also stressed that flexible response remained fully valid as long as there was no better alternative. He supported the basic concept of greater defense as part of alliance strategy, and hoped this could allow significant reductions in nuclear weapons. Unlike Reagan, however, he did not call for their elimination. Kohl also cited the importance of the economic and technological aspects of SDI. He argued that the European states should have the opportunity to participate in SDI research on an equal basis and not as part of a technological "one-way street." Such participation would give the Europeans an opportunity to gain greater influence over the SDI program, he said.

Kohl's most significant contribution to the SDI dialogue was the notion that SDI could enhance stability by moving NATO toward a combination of offensive and defensive weapons, a conception that went beyond any official U.S. thinking at the time. Most strikingly, he suggested that such a plan should be discussed with the Soviet Union and perhaps even placed on the negotiating table. By this statement, Kohl pointed the way toward a new strategic regime. This regime was to be based neither on mutual assured destruction, as had been planned under the ABM Treaty, nor on assured defense, as Reagan's 1983 speech had suggested, but on some combination that would preserve deterrence, stability, and concord among the superpowers. Kohl's suggestion was not at that time incorporated into American strategic thinking or into U.S. studies regarding the implications of strategic defense, although the United States later began to think in terms of a smaller defensive system.

Despite the doubts raised in Germany and elsewhere about the implications of a strategic defense system, some Germans—like many Americans—saw SDI as a way to preserve the effectiveness of extended deterrence by reducing U.S. vulnerability. Several German strategic analysts presented this argument before a special joint session about SDI of the *Bundestag* foreign and defense committees. The German analysts argued that when the United States was protected by a strategic defense system it would be more ready to use nuclear weapons in response to a Soviet invasion of Western Europe.[9] Franz-Josef Strauss, despite some reported reservations about SDI, also observed that a decrease in American vulnerability would make the American deterrent greater and "more infallible."[10]

France invited West Germany to participate in the EUREKA program for common European advanced technological research as a response to the technological benefits that the United States might derive from SDI, and West Germany began participating in a number of

EUREKA projects.[11] It also joined in various efforts to organize a collective West European response toward SDI.[12]

The Kohl Government knew of the growing concern of West German industry that it would fall behind the United States and Japan in the technological race. Despite some reservations about the role that they might be able to play, many German industrialists wished at least to explore what technological benefits SDI might offer.[13] Teltschik organized visits to Washington for German administrative and industrial figures.

On December 18, 1985, despite a personal letter from Gorbachev to Kohl, the Federal Republic formally decided to permit German firms to participate in the SDI program within the framework of an official German-American accord. Kohl sent Economics Minister Martin Bangemann to Washington to negotiate the terms for the participation of German firms.[14] He selected Bangemann to downplay the military aspects of SDI and stress that the German interest was primarily economic and technological. On March 27, 1986, Bangemann and Weinberger signed accords regulating German participation in SDI research. German industrial contracts in the first installment came to the level of $48.2 million, the largest total won by any West European country.[15]

Kohl again discussed SDI before the *Bundestag* on April 17, 1986. He used the occasion to reiterate his support for SDI as a research program but also to make some further comments on its potential strategic consequences.[16]

Kohl observed that the total elimination of nuclear weapons appeared unlikely but that it was entirely conceivable that a "new system of strategic stability" could be constructed. As part of this new system, both superpowers would agree on a "drastic reduction of nuclear offensive systems" and on the deployment of a "limited number of strategic defensive systems," perhaps only deployed on land (instead of in space). He warned that there might be risks involved in moving toward a new system of strategic stability from the present system of "overarmament" *(Ueberruestung)* and insisted that the security of the alliance as a whole had to be politically and strategically guaranteed.

Kohl thus presented a strategic concept that remained different from the American but that attempted to accept Reagan's proposal while preserving the traditional view of extended deterrence. He also gave much greater weight than Reagan to negotiations with the Soviet Union, further reinforcing Bonn's growing tendency throughout the latter 1980s to seek diplomatic as well as hardware solutions to security problems.

The Chancellor concluded with a statement containing four points that appeared best to summarize his government's approach:

- Security issues had to be seen and judged in connection with East-West relations. This also applied to SDI.
- Both superpowers were conducting research into ballistic missile defense, and the results of this research would alter the global strategic situation.
- In light of this, any defensive system would have to be drawn into a new cooperative security system between the two superpowers.
- Such a process carried some risks, and reducing them required alliance solidarity as well as the pursuit of common interests between East and West.

After Kohl's statement in the 1986 *Bundestag* debate, he and other members of his government said little about SDI or about strategic defense, although the Chancellor on December 10, 1987, when he formally welcomed the Soviet-American INF Treaty, recalled his earlier prediction that the world was heading toward a new strategic situation in which offense and defense would live side by side.[17]

The SDI issue stirred considerable debate in West Germany. The FDP was skeptical, although it supported the program in *Bundestag* votes. Genscher was more reserved than Kohl or Woerner about the possibility that new weapons developments might resolve problems that he perceived as essentially political and diplomatic. Most of all, he did not wish the new weapons, or the process of acquiring them, to disrupt the peace and stability that he believed the Federal Republic and its people had gained from the opening to the East. He warned that "a detente policy on earth and an arms race and confrontation in space cannot coexist."[18]

The two opposition parties in Germany, the SPD and the Greens, repeatedly denounced SDI. Horst Ehmke, the Social Democrats' strategic policy expert, criticized SDI during the *Bundestag* debate on April 18, 1985.[19] He recalled that the SPD had at first looked upon SDI with interest because it might supersede the concept of deterrence by mutual retaliation. However, he added, the SPD concluded that it would not support SDI. On May 23, 1985, former Chancellor Schmidt wrote to Kohl to argue strongly against West German government participation in SDI. Instead, he called for increased defense and economic cooperation with France.[20] The Green party consistently opposed SDI.

Ultimately, Bonn supported the SDI program because the government decided that West Germany could not oppose a program to which its principal ally was fully committed. Bonn also saw the possibility that some form of defense might be necessary to preserve extended deterrence. The German government hoped for some economic and scientific benefit, although its dimensions were unclear and appeared to diminish over time. But the main German theme was that any change in the global strategic regime should be discussed and agreed with Moscow in order to avoid disrupting global stability.

Bonn's search for a strategic concept that might bring SDI into the traditional NATO deterrence framework represented a significant German departure from its post-World War II reluctance to take independent positions on international strategic matters. It reflected at least a modest German readiness to explore strategic concepts on its own, even within the broad framework of a NATO strategy to which it remained fully committed. SDI thus left a legacy of having stimulated German thinking about strategic matters as profoundly as any development since the MLF debate of the 1960s. Even though nothing further came of the German proposals, that legacy was to mature in the latter 1980s into a new German readiness to speak and act more independently than before about strategic issues.

The Reykjavik Summit

Having barely put to rest the strategic questions posed by SDI, Bonn reacted in surprise and even consternation to the 1986 Reykjavik summit between Reagan and Gorbachev. There had been no advance NATO consultation on some of the most important elements of the summit, such as the sweeping discussion about eliminating nuclear missiles and nuclear weapons. Those aspects had raised questions even in the United States, but German officials could not understand how an American President who controlled the principal deterrent of the NATO alliance, surrounded by his most senior advisers, could even contemplate total elimination of the weapons that had made deterrence and peace possible. Although the summit achieved no formal agreement on strategic weapons, the discussions themselves were profoundly unsettling to West German strategists and officials.

For the Germans, Reykjavik meant that an American President had come perilously close to giving up the nuclear deterrent that defended West Germany and Berlin, leaving the Soviet Union militarily superior with its conventional forces on the European central front and elsewhere, and perhaps compelling the West into a ruinous conventional weapons competition that would significantly alter not only the economics but the politics of European security.

Bonn had on occasion had earlier misgivings about U.S. dealings with Moscow, just as Washington had its own worries about German *Ostpolitik*. Schmidt had reacted with disdain to President Carter's criticism of "the inordinate fear of Communism" and toward Secretary of State Cyrus Vance's first mission to Moscow in 1977. What made

Reykjavik different, however, was that an American President had been ready to deal so swiftly and unilaterally not only with strategic weapons numbers but with the very principles that Bonn saw at the heart of Western and German security. Coming after the SDI debate, it further added to German uncertainty about U.S. strategic thinking.

Many American officials were in turn surprised at the German reaction. They believed that they had achieved an important breakthrough by having reached a tentative accord isolating and forbidding nuclear ballistic missiles on a global basis. Washington has consistently regarded the first strike capacity of the heavy Soviet missiles, especially the SS-18s and SS-19s, as the principal threats to nuclear stability and even to extended deterrence. American officials believed that U.S. superiority in non-ballistic delivery vehicles, whether aircraft or cruise missiles, would count for more once ballistic missiles had been eliminated. But this mutual misunderstanding was never adequately clarified, and the West German reaction to the Reykjavik discussions remained negative.

If Bonn worried about Washington in the 1980s, Paris worried about Bonn. President François Mitterrand, like other French officials and analysts, had seen signs of potential neutralism in the German domestic debate and in popular opposition to the deployment of the Pershing II and the GLCM.[21] France, which did not suffer division, was never as fascinated by detente as the Germans, although it had its own relations with Moscow. After 1982, and especially after the SPD had turned against Schmidt, Paris accelerated its efforts to tie Germany more closely into a West European system that would counter what the French perceived as a dangerous German drift to the East. Henry Froment-Meurice in 1984 observed that "L'Allemagne bouge," reflecting French uneasiness about the emerging German mood.[22]

After Reykjavik, Bonn and Paris turned to each other (and, to a somewhat lesser degree, toward London as well). Paradoxically, Bonn turned to Paris because it wanted to have a connection that would be less susceptible than Washington to Gorbachev's diplomatic charm, a suspicion that Paris felt toward Bonn. Both watched each other, even as they watched the superpowers. Consultations intensified as did high-level visits. Franco-German discussions ranged into much broader areas of security cooperation than ever before, and those discussions were conducted at a higher level with both Mitterrand and Kohl personally and intensely involved. In fact, the good personal relationship between Kohl and Mitterrand became an important factor in Franco-German ties.

Bonn and Paris agreed to form a joint Franco-German Brigade of about 4,200 men, stationed in Germany and commanded alternately by a French or German general. To preserve the rule that *Bundeswehr* units had to be under NATO, the German elements of the brigade are to come from the territorial command. Nonetheless, to assure proper battlefield coordination, the unit is to operate under the operational control but not operational command of the Southern Territorial Command.[23] That would not put French forces into NATO, but it would still tie them directly into the defense of the German border.

Beyond the brigade, and even more significant in strategic terms, the · French government indicated a readiness to assist in the forward defense of the Federal Republic. France showed its intent by participating in the forward maneuver *Kecker Spatz*, an exercise to which U.S. observers were not invited. Declarations by Mitterrand and Premier Jacques Chirac in December 1987 committed France more firmly than before to the defense of German rather than only French territory. Chirac stated: "The survival of France is decided at its border and the security of France is decided at the borders of its neighbors." This was a much more categorical statement of the French interest in West German security than the French government had earlier been prepared to issue. Mitterrand, on a visit to Germany, reassured his German listeners that France, contrary to their previous quietly held fears, would not defend itself by detonating nuclear weapons on German soil, although he still reserved to the French government, and to that government alone, the decisions on the use of nuclear arms.[24]

Even before these events, France had been concerned about possible German fascination with the East. Both De Gaulle and Adenauer had feared such leanings, with Adenauer in particular mistrusting the Germans who might try to "dance between the two blocs." The two men had signed the original Elysée Treaty in 1963 in part to fight such temptations.[25]

France had already begun by the 1970s to conduct regular consultations with NATO, and certain operational understandings had been reached and had been intensified over the years. But the new Franco-German accords dwarfed any public steps that France had taken toward coordination with NATO. They represented a significant evolution in French and in German thinking. They were further advanced in October 1988 with an agreement for a joint France-German Defense and Security Council,[26] as well as with stepped-up Franco-German plans for joint weapons development and production.

Throughout its consultations and negotiations with France, Bonn feared that Washington's long-standing reservations about separate European arrangements within NATO or about any "European caucus" would make the United States oppose the Franco-German arrangement. German officials at all levels assured their American friends that the

new French link did not weaken NATO but strengthened it by asso-
ciating France more closely with the alliance. They also stressed that
it should have no effect on close links between the United States and
Western Europe.

The German State Secretary of Defense, Lothar Ruehl, wrote that
the new Franco-German ties constituted "a more solid foundation upon
which the European contribution to the common alliance defense can
be optimized," and that no "exclusive arrangements" had been made.[27]
Seeking to reassure not only Washington but also London and other
European capitals, he added that the Franco-German arrangement
constituted "neither a bid to challenge the alliance structure nor a
bilateral design for political dominance in Western Europe." He added
that it represented no "security alternative" to the American deterrence
guarantee. Bonn clearly did not want expanded Franco-German strategic
ties to break up European and Atlantic defense arrangements but to
reinforce them.[28]

Despite these assurances, Washington realized that the German moves
toward Paris represented a kind of insurance policy that reflected some
German doubts about the United States. A French guarantee did not
carry the same awesome weight in sheer megatonnage as a U.S. guarantee. But the development of her nuclear forces would give France—
like Great Britain—a significant deterrent by the year 2000. At a time
of uncertainty for Bonn, it represented a useful asset.

Kohl suggested carrying military collaboration with France further
than a bilateral relationship. He expressed himself strongly in favor of
a European army to advance West European integration and to improve
European defense cohesion and collaboration.[29] In an October 1988
speech, he argued that such an army should work in close collaboration
with the United States. Many observers, however, believed that his
European proposal, like the growing link with France, was primarily
intended to begin giving Western Europe the elements of its own defense
structure if the United States began to reduce its own commitments.

A number of European strategic analysts, including several Germans,
insisted that any European force would be more effective when linked
with the U.S. deterrent than with any other, but noted that such a force
would at least provide some defense if Moscow again became aggressive
and the American deterrent no longer shielded Europe.[30]

Kohl showed his own interest in Europe by turning to France in
reaction to both SDI and Reykjavik. His speeches and actions indicated
that he did not want to sever the German-American element in the
Federal Republic's security structure, but that he wanted to establish
at least the beginnings of a West European option. He might not prefer
that option, but he was ready to start preparing it if it should prove

necessary. The United States government looked on with some misgivings, but not enough to generate a shift in its own strategic thinking.

The Future of Deterrence: "Discriminate"?

In January 1988, after more than a year of study, an American special commission published a report, entitled *Discriminate Deterrence,* which purported to guide U.S. defense policy over the next twenty years.[31] The commission had two co-chairmen, Fred Iklé, then Undersecretary of Defense for Policy, and Albert Wohlstetter, the dean of American strategic planners. Every commission member, whether Anne Armstrong, Zbigniew Brzezinski, or Henry Kissinger, brought to the report not only a distinguished name but broad and intimate experience in strategic affairs at the highest level. Their presence on the commission conveyed the sense that the report was not only authoritative but definitive.

But the report suggested that Western Europe and the NATO link were no longer uniquely relevant to American security and that protecting them might not be worth excessive risk. The report devoted no special section to NATO, as it did to the third world, but instead listed a potential European conflict as merely one of a series of possible engagements "on the periphery of the Soviet Union." It suggested that Europe could perhaps be defended locally, and that deep strikes behind Warsaw Pact lines could deter and perhaps win a European war without the engagement of U.S. strategic forces. Those statements appeared to confirm SPD assertions that the United States would try to stay out of a European war and that U.S. nuclear weapons in Europe were not "coupling" but "de-coupling." Some Germans saw in it, as they had in SDI, Washington's determination to avoid risk-sharing.

The report dramatically transformed the nature of the NATO nuclear component and of its potential use. It specifically stated that NATO nuclear strikes should not be seen as a link to a wider and more devastating war—although it acknowledged that such a risk would of course remain—but "as an instrument for denying success to the invading Soviet forces."[32] Challenging the ambiguity that had been at the core of extended deterrence for over 20 years, it stated that the rules of engagement for nuclear weapons should be spelled out more clearly.

The report also warned against excess fascination with what it termed "extreme contingencies," such as a nuclear exchange that might be initiated at the start of a conflict or that might grow out of escalation from conventional war—scenarios that many strategic planners envisaged at the start of a potential war in Europe. It warned that such contingencies had gained too firm a hold on strategic thinking, especially in Europe, and that defense planners should focus on "more plausible" contingencies. It warned against making nuclear threats that were "apocalyptic."

The *Discriminate Deterrence* report, like SDI and the Reykjavik summit, further contributed to the West European—and especially West German—belief that American strategic thinking was moving away from the principles that had helped to establish and maintain Atlantic security. That impression was reinforced by the commission's ill-defined relation to official U.S. policy. It had a senior U.S. official as its co-chairman and it had a large number of serving U.S. military officers (but no State Department officials) on its staff. Like SDI and Reykjavik, it therefore raised questions about the trends of official U.S. security planning. Some Germans saw it as a trial balloon that reflected U.S. official thinking but was published in a manner that made it deniable.

The more the West Germans read the report, the more baffled they became. They saw no link to traditional NATO strategy but also saw no clear acknowledgement that the United States wished to depart from that strategy. They concluded that the report had to reflect changes in U.S. thinking or at least informed speculation by senior statesmen trying to reconcile the obligations of the post-war era with the shifting realities of the strategic balance and the expanding global demands being placed upon U.S. resources. Unable to conclude what it might mean for the future, they nonetheless feared that it appeared to expose Germany and Europe to a separate confrontation with the Soviet empire.

Three leading West European strategic analysts, including one German, wrote a brief but widely published response in which they criticized the *Discriminate Deterrence* report on four counts:

1. That some perception of the danger of global nuclear escalation must remain to avoid potential miscalculation leading to a war in Europe.
2. That the Soviets should not be invited to believe that a war in Europe would remain conventional.
3. That any suggestion of a "strategic counteroffensive" against the Warsaw Pact in Europe would be highly counterproductive to Western efforts at better relations with Eastern Europe.
4. That U.S. strategic thinking should at least give Western Europe the status of a separate strategic entity.[33]

Although the three European commentators were private citizens, the tone and content of their article suggested that it reflected official— and especially German—views. As if to underscore this, other European and German comment echoed these themes. Lothar Ruehl, Iklé's German counterpart, warned that the report left Europe no choice but to take "more responsibility for its defense with its own forces."[34]

The authors of *Discriminate Deterrence* replied that the Europeans had misunderstood their paper.[35] They said that they certainly envisaged the use of intercontinental as well as European-based nuclear forces to respond to any attack on NATO Europe, and that the response should be aimed at targets in the Soviet Union as well as in Eastern Europe. They argued that they had wanted to make certain that the use of nuclear weapons was discriminate and effective, but they certainly had not intended to rule out any use of strategic forces. They also stated that the indiscriminate use of nuclear forces to repel aggression could risk destroying Europe, and that it had been their intent to point this out. They concluded by welcoming a larger British and French nuclear role and suggesting that those countries should also develop nuclear forces that could be used with discrimination.

Doubts and Options

As the 1980s drew to a close, German officials and defense analysts came gradually to the conclusion that the role of extended deterrence in U.S. strategic policy had become increasingly fuzzy, not because the United States seemed to be walking away from its commitments but because those commitments were not at the forefront of American senior-level thinking. Although U.S. officials reiterated the commitments often and forcefully, what bothered the Germans was that the United States also pursued policies or took actions that appeared to be inconsistent with NATO strategic doctrine.

With their traditional yearning for logical consistency, a tradition not shared or even understood by many Americans, the Germans found it difficult to conceive that U.S. officials might remain firmly committed to extended deterrence even as they took actions or wrote papers that appeared to depart from that policy.

American officials in turn complained privately that the Germans should not think that the American government had abandoned extended deterrence just because U.S. officials did not swear allegiance to it at least once a week. Recalling Congressional criticism regarding European burden-sharing, some U.S. officials said that it would even be better if the U.S. commitment to Western Europe were not paraded too forcefully. U.S. officials concerned with SDI also complained that Germans tended to see a weakening of U.S. deterrence strategy in actions—like SDI—that would reinforce it.

Bonn reacted in several ways to its uncertainty about U.S. strategy. Principally, the German government tried to persuade the United States to maintain deterrence and to state so clearly. At the same time, it tried to find a European alternative that Moscow would respect but that would not alienate the United States. It also continued and expanded its diplomatic efforts to reduce the possibility of conflict in the first place by improving relations with the Soviet Union. Here, again, Bonn tried to supplement military security with security sought by diplomacy.

The German-American dialogue on these points, however, made some strange bedfellows. In the past, most German and American strategic planners had agreed with each other about the essential elements of alliance security, and they had supported each other in their respective domestic debates. But during the 1980s many American supporters of NATO defense complained about German refusal to support U.S. actions outside the NATO area, and many German supporters of NATO were among those who most sharply criticized the Reykjavik summit or the *Discriminate Deterrence* report. Thus, actions taken by the United States or the Federal Republic were criticized in the other country by those persons who were normally most firmly committed to good German-American relations and to close security collaboration. Both countries were taking steps that disturbed their friends in the other.

But the arguments during the mid-1980s about various U.S. policies faded in significance by the end of the decade when Bonn and Washington at times disagreed even more openly about the instruments of deterrence and their use. These problems no longer drew the attention only of strategic or political experts but of broad circles of public opinion in both countries. They went to the heart of military and diplomatic policy, and they were to create even greater problems for the continued coordination of German-American as well as NATO strategy.

Notes

1. Karl Kaiser, "SDI und deutsche Politik," *Europa-Archiv,* Nov. 19, 1986, p. 569; Keith Payne, *Strategic Defense* (Lanham, Md.: Hamilton Press, 1986), pp. 194–195.

2. Kaiser, "SDI und deutsche Politik," p. 570. A summary of German reservations is in Dean Godson, *SDI: Has America told her Story to the World?* (Washington: Pergamon-Brassey's, 1987), p. 65.

3. Kaiser, "SDI und deutsche Politik," p. 570.

4. *FBIS, Western Europe,* April 10, 1984, pp. J1–J2.

5. Kaiser, "SDI und deutsche Politik," p. 570.

6. The Soviet line on this was reflected in excerpts quoted in *Europa-Archiv,* October 25, 1985, pp. 566–571.

7. Kaiser, "SDI und deutsche Politik," p. 572.

8. Bundesministerium der Verteidigung, *SDI: Fakten und Bewertungen, Fragen und Antworten; Dokumentation* (Bonn: Ministry of Defense, 1986) pp. 53–58.

9. Jaquelyn K. Davis and Robert L. Pfaltzgraff, Jr., *Strategic Defense and Extended Deterrence* (Cambridge, Mass.: Institute for Foreign Policy Analysis, 1986), pp. v–viii. For the German analysis, see remarks of Michael Stuermer and Uwe Nerlich in Deutscher Bundestag, 10. Wahlperiode, "Stenographisches Protokoll der Sitzung des Auswaertigen Ausschusses und des Verteidigungsausschusses, December 9-10, 1985."

10. Ivo H. Daalder, *The SDI Challenge to Europe* (Cambridge, Mass.: Ballinger, 1987), p. 39.

11. Robert E. Osgood, "The Implications of SDI for U.S.-European Relations," Robert W. Tucker, George Liska, Robert Osgood, David Calleo, *SDI and U.S. Foreign Policy* (Boulder, Colo.: Westview Press, 1986), p. 87.

12. *Ibid.*

13. Klaus Achmann, "Forschungsbeteiligung am SDI-Projekt," Hartmut Buehl, Ed., *Strategiediskussion* (Bonn: E.S. Mittler & Sohn, 1987), p. 363.

14. Bundesministerium der Verteidigung, *SDI: Fakten und Bewertungen,* p. 61, prints text of the West German decision.

15. U.S. Strategic Defense Initiative Organization, "Report to the Congress of the United States," April, 1987, p. B–4.

16. Text of the Chancellor's statement is in Presse- und Informationsamt der Bundesregierung, "Pressemitteilung," April 17, 1986. Also see *Bulletin,* April 18, 1987, pp. 305–308.

17. Speech distributed by the German Information Service, New York, December 12, 1987.

18. *FBIS, Western Europe,* May 20, 1985, p. J1.

19. Bundestag, *Protokoll,* April 18, 1985, pp. 9720–9727.

20. Samuel F. Wells, Jr., "The SDI, Eureka, and European Cooperation," Dan Quayle, Robert E. Hunter, C. Elliott Farmer, *Strategic Defense and the Western Alliance* (Washington: Center for Strategic and International Studies, 1986), p. 32.

21. Robert M. Beecroft, "France, the FRG, and European Defense," unpublished paper prepared for the National Defense University, Washington, March, 1988, pp. 20–21.

22. Michael Stuermer, "Franco-German Relations Past and Present," a paper presented to the Washington European Seminar, Center for Strategic and International Studies, Washington, May 12, 1988, p. 10.

23. *Frankfurter Allgemeine,* January 23, 1988, p. 2.

24. Jolyon Howorth, "Die Franzoesische Verteidingungspolitik im Widerstreit zwischen Abruestung und Abschreckung," *Europa-Archiv,* June 25, 1988, pp. 334–335.

25. Stuermer, "Franco-German Relations," p. 10.

26. "Deutschland-Nachrichten," October 19, 1988.

27. Lothar Ruehl, "Franco-German Military Cooperation: An Insurance Policy for the Alliance," *Strategic Review,* Summer, 1988, pp. 48–54.

28. François Heisbourg, "Nach dem INF-Abkommen von Washington: Fuer eine Weiterentwicklung der Grundlagen des Atlantischen Buendnisses," *Europa-Archiv,* March 10, 1988, p. 126.

29. *Financial Times,* October 14, 1988.

30. *Wall Street Journal,* February 17, 1989.

31. The Commission on Long-Term Integrated Strategy, *Discriminate Deterrence* (Washington: U.S. Government Printing Office, 1988).

32. Commission on Long-Term Strategy, *Discriminate Deterrence,* see pp. 29–37 for concepts and citations reported here.

33. *International Herald Tribune,* February 1, 1988. A German version is in *Europa-Archiv,* March 10, 1988, pp. 129–131.

34. *Die Welt,* January 19, 1988.

35. The response, written by Brzezinski, Kissinger, Iklé and Wohlstetter, appeared in *International Herald Tribune,* February 24, 1988.

5

Strategy Under Challenge

The INF Missiles Deployed

Chancellor Schmidt shocked Washington in October 1977 when he publicly warned that the Western alliance was failing to provide the instruments needed to implement its strategy of extended deterrence. That speech was one of the most important turning points in alliance discussions regarding the missile balance in and around Europe, a problem that has dominated German-American strategic collaboration since the early 1970s and that is now forcing an entirely new look at NATO strategy.

Schmidt, like many other German strategists, was disturbed by Soviet deployment of a new mobile missile with three warheads, the SS-20, whose range of 5,500 kilometers covered all of Europe. The new missiles could clearly intimidate NATO Europe, giving Moscow potential escalation control in any European engagement. They could strike any country in Europe at any time of Moscow's choosing, could not be destroyed before launch because they were mobile, and could paralyze any NATO response to a Warsaw Pact attack.

The deployment of Soviet INF missiles followed a long period of steady growth in Soviet ICBMs, shorter-range nuclear missile forces (SNF), and conventional equipment in Eastern Europe.[1] During all this time, the MBFR talks were droning on in Vienna and the West European strategic community was becoming increasingly uneasy. It appeared that the Soviet Union was beginning to outnumber and outgun NATO forces at every level, intercontinental and European, without cutting its conventional superiority, and that this would significantly weaken NATO security. The changes in each area had become so great that, in combination, they shifted the fundamentals of the East-West balance and raised questions about the credibility of deterrence and the effectiveness of European defense.

The Germans perceived the SS-20 missile as the most serious security problem facing the NATO alliance because it could paralyze flexible response. From 1976 through most of 1977, German analysts and officials repeatedly expressed their worries to their American and other NATO colleagues, at Bonn or Brussels, but did not believe that they received the attention that their warnings deserved.

German alarm about the new missiles thus came to a head in Schmidt's speech, in which he warned sternly against the potential consequences of the new Soviet deployments. He stated that NATO "must be ready to make available the means to support its present strategy, which is still the right one, and to prevent any developments that could undermine the basis of this strategy." The speech created a sensation in NATO circles as in Washington because it reflected a crisis within the alliance about the ability and the determination of the West—and specifically of the United States—to maintain the balance and the peace of Europe.

Schmidt's speech led to urgent NATO consultations and studies. NATO members generally agreed that the alliance had to take action to match the Soviet build-up. They chose to deploy two new U.S. missile systems in Western Europe, 108 Pershing II launchers and 464 Ground-Launched Cruise Missiles (GLCM), weapons that were themselves mobile and that had a high probability of penetrating Soviet defenses. The cruise missiles could reach Moscow. The Pershing II missiles could not reach Moscow itself but could penetrate deeply into Soviet territory. They were the more fearsome weapons with their high accuracy, great speed, and virtually assured penetration capacity. They were the first U.S. ballistic missiles that could reach Soviet territory from a European NATO state since the withdrawal of the Jupiter missiles from Turkey after the 1962 Cuban missile crisis. Pershing launchers were to be deployed largely in West Germany, unleashing a series of harsh Soviet threats addressed specifically at the West German government and population. Soviet doctrine saw the missiles as strategic weapons.

Many West European and West German political figures and parties opposed deployment of the new NATO weapons even as the Soviet build-up continued. The German anti-nuclear movement was joined by portions of the SPD and by the Greens in its opposition to the new weapons. They warned that stationing the weapons in Germany would sweep away the remnants of detente, terminate whatever prospects remained for arms control, and risk a Soviet nuclear attack against Western Europe and specifically against the deployment sites in the Federal Republic. The opposition was so powerful that the West German government stated from the beginning that it could not be the only country on the continent to station the new weapons. As with the

MLF fifteen years earlier, it insisted that it could deploy only if others also did.

To demonstrate to the world that the alliance was prepared to use diplomacy to try to reestablish a balance, several states urged that NATO offer to stop deployment of the new weapons if the Soviet Union would withdraw the SS-20s. NATO in 1979 decided to incorporate that offer into its deployment decision. In 1981, it formally proposed the "zero option," under which neither side was to keep any of the intermediate-range missiles. It was never made clear whether NATO offered the zero option because it really wanted to eliminate the missiles or because it thought Moscow would not accept it. Different persons probably had different motives, in Bonn and Washington. Moscow refused to negotiate but walked out of the Geneva arms control negotiations.[2] The Soviets had reason to expect that public protests would stop NATO INF deployment while leaving the Soviet missiles in place.

Opposition in the NATO countries was violent. The protests were to culminate in 1983, before the beginning of actual deployment, in what the German anti-nuclear movement promised would be a *"Heisser Herbst"*—a "Hot Autumn." Nonetheless, deployment proceeded and the demonstrations proved to be less well attended and less effective than expected. The new West German government of Chancellor Kohl stood firmly by the NATO decision. It was supported by Genscher's FDP, which had left the coalition with the SPD and had joined Kohl to form the new German government when Schmidt was denounced and forced to resign by his own party for having helped launch the NATO deployment.

The domestic German debate about INF deployment opened many old wounds. It was not the first time that West German public opinion had reacted strongly and negatively to the stationing of nuclear weapons in West Germany, but the INF protest left new and deeper scars. Just as the Germans questioned U.S. determination to maintain deterrence, Americans now questioned Germany's ability to sustain the obligations of nuclear burden-sharing. The deployment protest also showed how Moscow could wreak havoc in Western opinion, deploying forces almost at will without any protest—Western or Eastern—whereas the matching NATO deployments were blocked, delayed, or at least harassed by violent demonstrators.

The INF Missile Accord

From 1983 to 1985, the INF deployment proceeded in NATO Europe while the Soviet Union refused to negotiate. After Gorbachev came to power, however, Moscow quickly resumed diplomatic activity. First,

Gorbachev and Reagan discussed broad questions of Soviet-American relations and arms control at Geneva in 1985. A year later, in their meeting at Reykjavik, they not only made proposals for global nuclear arms control but also agreed in general terms to the reduction of Soviet and American missiles with a range between 500 and 5,500 kilometers.

A number of elements of the INF agreement still remained to be negotiated but were settled rather quickly by arms control standards. After some discussion, Moscow accepted the zero option, agreeing to world-wide elimination of the missiles. Moscow and Washington agreed on arrangements governing verification and enforcement of the treaty provisions. The United States consulted closely with European NATO countries, especially West Germany, since the measures would come into force mainly in Europe.

As the negotiations advanced, however, the Federal Republic had reservations. German military strategists and some politicians complained privately in Bonn and Washington about the treaty's lower range limit of 500 (instead of 1,000) kilometers because it would prevent NATO from deploying missiles that could reach beyond German territory and because it would compel NATO to station all or virtually all its present and future missiles on German soil.[3] The United States NATO arsenal then had no missiles in the 500 to 1,000 kilometer range, but the Federal Republic possessed seventy-two older Pershing IA missiles of 720 kilometer range that could carry American nuclear warheads. The United States did not accept the German reservations and may not even have understood the seriousness with which they were held because they were not vigorously advanced at the senior political level and were often raised in informal rather than formal exchanges. Washington officials also believed, like German officials, that any INF agreement would not limit German (or French and British) missiles as it was to apply only to Soviet and American weapons.

The Soviets seemed to pay little attention to the Pershing IA missiles during most of the INF talks, and the German government wanted and expected to keep the missiles. However, as the INF negotiations neared completion, Moscow suddenly insisted that those missiles also had to be removed for a true zero solution.

The German government asserted that it should be able to keep the Pershing IA missiles as they were not American-controlled and therefore not within the scope of the talks. It hoped that Washington would support its position, but Washington said that this was a matter for the German government itself to decide. The Germans could not take it upon themselves to jeopardize a potentially significant East-West arms control agreement for the sake of a relatively small number of old missiles. Kohl agreed that the Pershing IA missiles would be destroyed in conjunction with other INF missiles, although the provisions regarding their destruction would not be part of the INF accord itself. Nonetheless, the matter left considerable bitterness in the German government which would have preferred to keep the missiles and which had believed that the United States supported this view.[4]

The West German government and strategic community thus reacted with strikingly mixed feelings after the INF agreement was signed during the Reagan-Gorbachev Washington summit of December 1987. The official reaction was one of enthusiastic approval, especially in the Foreign Ministry and its arms control office. The German military, however, had reservations, as did a number of West German defense analysts. Behind the official approval lay considerable uncertainty and even concern about the potentially negative effect of the treaty on NATO and German security, and about the impact that removal of the Western missiles would have on the totality of NATO strategy.

The INF agreement had obvious and significant advantages. The SS-20s that had jeopardized extended deterrence were to be destroyed. A total of over 3,000 Soviet warheads would be eliminated, in contrast to about 800 U.S./NATO warheads (as well as the Pershing IAs). Moscow had accepted the principles of asymmetrical reductions and intrusive verification, principles that the West had long sought because they were essential to future arms control agreements and especially to conventional force reductions. Many Germans believed, moreover, that the INF agreement was important not only for itself but as a first step toward further agreements that would help stabilize the global and European balances and reduce international tension. Kohl and Genscher spoke very positively about the accord.

The disadvantages of the agreement were also real but much harder to analyze precisely. The agreement removed two types of weapons that could hit Soviet territory and were, therefore, uniquely effective instruments of extended deterrence. In contrast, especially after the departure of the Pershing IA, it left missiles that could to all practical purposes hit only German soil, West or East. Moreover, even as it eliminated one area of Soviet superiority, it left such others as the conventional imbalance and a considerable Soviet advantage in short-range nuclear missiles. Woerner publicly expressed some reservations about the treaty, as did some military analysts. Admiral Dieter Wellershoff, the Inspector General of the German armed forces, warned that the treaty would result in the loss of "some important military options."[5]

The main German worry was the Soviet advantage in short-range missile forces (SNF). Even after the destruction of the INF missiles, the Warsaw Pact retained about 1350 missile launchers with a range below 500 kilometers: The SCUD-B (350 kilometers), the SS-21 (120 kilometers), and the older FROG (70 kilometers). If one were to draw a line along the outer limits of the potential striking range of the SCUD-B from sites in East Germany and Czechoslovakia, it would coincide almost exactly, as if by design, with the western border of the Federal Republic. Those missiles, could therefore inhibit German decision-making and defense preparations. The shorter-range missiles, such as the SS-21 and the FROG, could make forward defense virtually impossible because they could strike the first NATO defense lines as well as some rear installations. With modern conventional warheads, the missiles could paralyze NATO airfields in Germany without initiating a nuclear conflict. Only 88 of the corresponding Western missile launcher, the 110-kilometer Lance, remained available to NATO.

The threat to NATO was not quite as dramatic as the 14-1 ratio suggested. Not all Soviet and other Warsaw Pact launchers, with their replacement missiles, have been positioned to strike NATO territory. Many face Asia and the Middle East. Opposite NATO, not all face West Germany. Nonetheless, with their normal complement of several missiles for each launcher, even the launchers that might at any moment be in Eastern Europe could alone fire hundreds of nuclear or conventional warheads at West Germany from distances up to several hundred kilometers. The Lance missile, in turn, could only strike 110 kilometers away.

West German analysts, journalists, strategists and politicians warned about the "singularization" of Germany after the INF accord. Senior CDU officials like Alfred Dregger and Volker Ruehe appeared in Washington during 1987 and 1988 to underline this problem. Many Germans repeated a slogan: "The shorter the missiles, the deader the Germans." They warned that short-range weapons and warheads remaining on German territory, such as nuclear artillery, were "self-deterring" because a West German government could not agree that NATO precipitate the destruction they would bring upon the German nation, East and West.[6]

In their criticism of the INF accord, few Germans seemed to remember that their own government had supported and even initiated the zero option. Instead, they focused their criticism almost entirely upon the United States which negotiated and signed it, and which had done so with what had appeared officially to be full and even enthusiastic German approval.

SNF Modernization

Even before the INF agreement had been signed and ratified, German-American and NATO discussion began to concentrate on the next steps to be taken. One of the steps proposed most vigorously by the United States was the upgrading of the 88 Lance launchers to give them greater range and precision.

The U.S. proposal was based on plans made several years before the INF accord was negotiated and signed. In October 1983, while no East-West negotiations were under way, the NATO Nuclear Planning Group had already agreed at Montebello that its nuclear arsenal needed modernization. That modernization program was proceeding, replacing older warheads and launch equipment—such as nuclear artillery—with more efficient and effective materiel.[7] The United States and Great Britain insisted that the Montebello program should continue to be carried out, especially as it pre-dated the INF accord and had been designed to meet basic alliance tactical and strategic requirements.

But West German officials and political figures began to express some reservations about the Montebello process, especially because the short-range weapons that were to be modernized suddenly appeared in a new light as part of the whole complex of "singularization" and because of deepening West German opposition to nuclear weapons.

Chancellor Kohl himself seized the issue with an interview to the *Financial Times* in which he stated that there was no reason to rush Lance modernization, as the Lance missiles in the inventory would not be obsolete until after 1995 and no decision needed to be made before 1991 or 1992.[8] Kohl clearly wanted time to evaluate other strategic and political developments. More important, given the 1981–1983 anti-INF riots and demonstrations that Germans still remembered all too well, the decision would be postponed until after the next West German national election, scheduled for December 1990.

Kohl's decision aroused concern in Washington and London. The new U.S. Secretary of State, James Baker, urged Kohl in Bonn to permit an early NATO decision. British Prime Minister Margaret Thatcher used the occasion of a meeting with Kohl to make similar arguments. Kohl, however, continued to demur. The Soviet Union also chimed in, with Foreign Minister Eduard Shevardnadze warning that a Lance modernization decision would force Moscow to reconsider destroying the SS-23 missiles to be scrapped under the INF Treaty. Moscow later withdrew that threat.[9]

By the NATO 40th anniversary meeting in May, 1989, it was clear that Kohl would not change his position, and that any modernization decision would have to be postponed. By then it was also clear that his view had wide support across the German political spectrum, whether from the SPD or conservative elements of the CDU, and from many other NATO states.[10]

The decision to postpone Lance modernization leaves a number of problems for the alliance, especially because the Soviet Union could replace some of the functions of the SS-20s and other condemned missiles with new weapons of its own such as the mobile SS-24 and SS-25 missiles—which appear to have primarily an intercontinental mission but which could also target Western Europe as the SS-20 did. The Soviet Union has reportedly been testing short-range missile prototypes that could replace or modernize the SCUD-B, the SS-21, and the FROG, and is also stationing Yankee class submarines in the seas off Western Europe in such a way that their missiles could threaten a number of NATO countries.[11] The combination of such missiles, if deployed and so targeted, could re-establish some of the intimidation that the SS-20s possessed and that the INF treaty was intended to eliminate.

A more serious problem, however, is to find a means to bridge the gap between the short-range weapons and the intercontinental systems in order to maintain extended deterrence. The systems should be credible enough to serve as a deterrent, but not so inviting that they give West European states the sense that they might be selected as special targets. They must also overcome the German fear of "singularization."

Although a decision was postponed at the 40th NATO anniversary summit, and may not be needed if further arms control can establish a European balance without further weapons, many political and military figures believed that NATO, the United States, and the Federal Republic must be prepared at least to understand and to review a number of possible options for SNF modernization if it should prove necessary:

- A system of tactical air-to-surface missiles (TASMs), to be fired from U.S. and other NATO aircraft. They would have ranges below 500 kilometers but, since they would be carried by penetration aircraft, could strike targets well beyond East Germany.
- A follow-on ground-based system, as a direct successor to the Lance, perhaps in the form of nuclear missiles to be fired from the Multiple-Launcher Rocket System (MLRS). Those missiles must have a range below 500 kilometers because of the INF treaty, but they would still have a greater reach than the Lance and could strike beyond German territory.
- Stepped-up production, and possible deployment in the European NATO area, of Submarine-Launched Cruise Missiles (SLCMs). They would match greater Soviet submarine deployment off Western Europe. Their range could be greater than 500 kilometers since they are not forbidden by the INF treaty as GLCMs above that range have been.

- Deployment to the European NATO area of some bombers or fighter-bombers carrying Air-Launched Cruise Missiles (ALCMs).
- In addition, because of the greater deterrent role of NATO airfields after the deployment of additional nuclear-capable aircraft, NATO might need an anti-tactical ballistic missile (ATBM) defense system to protect those airfields from Soviet missiles.[12]

These steps need not bring more nuclear warheads to Europe. They could and probably would be accompanied by a reduction in the number of artillery or other short-range weapons, almost certainly in greater number than the new ones to be deployed.[13] The purpose of the new weapons would not be to increase the number of nuclear warheads but to change the type of weapon to one that would not be self-deterred and to conform with current military and political needs of the alliance, especially the Germans.

The German government, however, became progressively more concerned about opposition than about singularization. The SPD, the Greens, and several anti-nuclear groups signalled their intent to oppose any plans for deployment of new nuclear weapons in West Germany. And any German government planning nuclear modernization might be split by the resulting controversy, not only between different parties but within them.

Modernization would be particularly difficult because of the very positive impact of Soviet arms control and reduction proposals and announcements on German and general Western opinion. Those proposals and announcements would not be fully implemented until well into the 1990s, but they make a powerful political impression well before they make a military difference. Moscow can also threaten to withdraw them to retaliate against a NATO decision that it finds distasteful. In the meantime, they complicate Western and especially German decision-making, stimulating objections from both the Right and the Left although for different reasons.

Whatever decision may ultimately be made, NATO and the Federal Republic face a "window of singularity" of at least several years because the retirement of the Pershings and GLCMs must be completed by 1991. Then, without actual modernization having taken place, the longest range for missiles in the Western arsenal would be 110 kilometers whereas the Warsaw Pact would have 350 kilometers and perhaps more later. Even at best, this disparity could not be corrected for a number of years.

Arms Control Disputes

Washington's concern about Bonn's refusal to agree to early Lance modernization had barely begun to subside when the German government shook the alliance with yet another separate proposal in April 1989. The Federal Republic asked for U.S. and NATO agreement for East-West talks about reducing the short-range SNF systems that the Germans found "singularizing."

Kohl sent Genscher and the newly appointed Defense Minister, Gerhard Stoltenberg, to propose that the NATO summit offer East-West negotiations on reducing those short-range systems, including not only the Lance but especially nuclear artillery and similar systems.[14] The United States rejected the German idea, with Baker's spokesman announcing that the Secretary thought it would be a "mistake" to negotiate about such systems.[15] Washington believed that Kohl was more motivated by domestic political than strategic considerations. The Germans in turn argued that Soviet superiority was so overwhelming that negotiations could only help the West. They also stated that they wanted to show that "Bonn has something important to contribute" to alliance discussions.[16]

One reason Washington was so disturbed by the proposal was the fear that it would lead to yet another "zero option," leaving no nuclear weapons on the ground in continental Europe and thus compelling U.S. forces to serve without the nuclear weapons they might need to deter attack. American Senators spoke of withdrawing troops on the basis of "no nukes, no troops." German officials, at least initially, stated that they would not propose and would not even agree to total elimination of short-range nuclear weapons.

The dispute was widely described as the most serious that had faced NATO in many years, if not since the beginning, because it raised so many delicate questions between two states that anchored the NATO strategic structure. Other NATO states took sides, with Great Britain supporting the United States but most other NATO states agreeing with Bonn.

The German-American dispute threatened to provoke a major confrontation at the 40th Anniversary NATO summit, a risk averted only by Bush's personal intervention. The President shifted the U.S. position on arms control, linking conventional and SNF negotiations and thus meeting the German need for nuclear negotiations and the U.S. need for reductions in Moscow's conventional threat. He modified the U.S. position on European conventional arms control by agreeing to include strike aircraft in the talks, boosting chances for early progress. He proposed a common ceiling of 275,000 U.S. and Soviet soldiers in Europe (outside Russian territory). He agreed to negotiations on nuclear SNF systems. He made it clear that he still wished conventional reductions to begin before nuclear SNF negotiations, but as a further concession to Bonn's desire for early talks he called for faster progress in the conventional talks themselves. This also had the advantage of smoking out Soviet intentions before the middle 1990s.[17]

NATO agreement on Bush's proposals solved the immediate German-American dispute but did not put the issue completely to rest. Bush left Brussels for a highly successful tour of West Germany, in which he made a speech reiterating the NATO proposals. He added that he understood the "special burden" of the nuclear weapons for West Germany but added that "in this nuclear age, every nation is on the front line."[18]

Despite Bush's plans and his visit, a number of German officials indicated that they would not be prepared to wait indefinitely for some progress in conventional arms talks before starting negotiations about SNF, and they also refused to rule out a possible "zero option" on the short-range systems in Germany.[19] Genscher took pride in the success of Germany's pressures on the United States and other NATO countries, informing the *Bundestag* that he would not underestimate the Federal Republic's importance in bringing about the NATO proposals.[20] In Washington, however, officials remained deeply disturbed at the implications of the German proposals for NATO strategy.

Arms Control Prospects

The 1990s may well become the decade of arms control, for Europe and beyond, when the Warsaw Pact and NATO make a major effort to reduce the weapons and forces facing each other in Europe while Washington and Moscow try simultaneously to reduce their strategic arsenals. If all goes according to plan, the decade should witness at least two and perhaps three major successful arms control negotiations that should directly or indirectly affect German and American security. And, if Bonn and Washington properly conceive and coordinate their common interests, arms control should reinforce their common security.

The principal arms control talks that now include both Bonn and Washington are the Conventional Forces in Europe (CFE) talks that began in Vienna in 1989. Those talks had not been expected to make very rapid progress because the issues were highly complicated and there was no immediate compromise visible between Western and Soviet positions. But NATO announced at the 40th anniversary summit that major progress should be made by 1990 with significant mutual reductions to begin in the early 1990s, which should give some impetus to the negotiations.

The Soviet Union has made some proposals that include a readiness to exchange data and to accept a serious inspection regime.[21] It has also said that it wishes to reach agreements that would identify and eliminate disparities, reduce forces on both sides to a level about one third below the present lowest levels, and give all forces a "defensive character." Gorbachev has already announced a unilateral withdrawal of six armored divisions from the GDR, Czechoslovakia, and Hungary over two years. He has added that the Soviet Union would reduce tank, artillery, and aircraft numbers in Europe, and that Soviet forces in Eastern Europe would be so reorganized as to be "clearly defensive." Several other Warsaw Pact governments, including the GDR, have also announced unilateral troop reductions.[22] Such Soviet conventional arms reductions could have a direct impact on NATO plans, capacities, and/or requirements, and could also affect German-American strategic planning.

To date, NATO proposals have been formulated to avoid reducing NATO forces in Germany below the number necessary for maintaining a strong defensive position. NATO has proposed reductions that would bring both NATO and Warsaw Pact forces, as well as American and Soviet forces, into balance at lower levels than the present Western forces. These proposals have not to date matched Gorbachev's for popular appeal. Nor is it clear what impact the combination of these proposals would have not only on the East-West confrontation but also on Moscow's ability to control developments in Eastern and Central Europe—if indeed that remains a Soviet interest.

Even though the CFE talks are officially about conventional weapons, they could have an impact on the nuclear deterrent and also on broad NATO plans. Western attack aircraft and helicopters are to be included in the talks, which could reduce the number of aircraft available for nuclear strike missions and could complicate arrangements to deliver nuclear weapons by air beyond German territory. Moscow has indicated that it wants to include naval units in negotiations on the conventional balance. Naval vessels have no ability to affect a land battle except indirectly, and do not represent the same threat to Moscow or Warsaw that tanks represent to Bonn or Hamburg. They do, however, have important reinforcement missions that link the United States to European operations. Moscow has also proposed counting stocks of equipment in storage for reinforcement units, although Soviet contingency forces would not need such pre-storage as much as U.S. forces. Such Soviet conventional reduction proposals have a strategic thrust as well as an arms control purpose, a thrust intended to weaken trans-Atlantic links and therefore German-American strategic collaboration.

The Federal Republic has made some proposals of its own for conventional arms control.[23] It has stated that the main reductions should be in tanks, other armored combat vehicles, and heavy artillery, and that the negotiations should focus on large military units. It has proposed limits on logistical support capacity and on the speed with which troop reinforcements could be deployed. It also wants to place a limit on total troop strength. These proposals, if implemented, should limit the capacity of Warsaw Pact conventional forces to attack and penetrate West German territory. They are in line with Bonn's traditional attachment to forward defense.

The Federal Republic faces another type of "singularization" in the conventional arms talks, however, because Paris has been unwilling to let its forces be treated along with other NATO forces in the talks. The German delegation was disturbed when the French Foreign Minister in early 1989 again singled out West German and Benelux territory as a special zone.[24] The Soviets have spoken of the "Austrian model" as a possible result of the conventional arms reduction talks. Some of these remarks hint at a potential limit on forces in West Germany, a consistent Soviet objective during the MBFR negotiations and one that could severely limit West Germany's capacity to respond to changes in the European security situation.

Another set of negotiations beginning in 1989 are the Strategic Arms Reduction Talks (START) between Washington and Moscow. They are operating under the general guidelines agreed by Reagan and Gorbachev at Reykjavik for 50 per cent reductions. The talks cover a number of issues not of direct concern to German-American security relations, but they could affect those relations if a 50 per cent reduction is strategic forces limits the weapons that the United States could commit to extended deterrence. By the same token, other global negotiations—such as those on chemical weapons—would also have effects in Europe although not principally upon German-American security ties.

Beyond these negotiations, SNF talks could begin early in the 1990s. Bonn has continued to press for these talks. Moscow, sensing that this issue could divide NATO, has stepped up its own rhetoric. Gorbachev used his visit to Paris in July 1989 to push for early talks, but neither he nor other Soviet officials have indicated that they were prepared to follow the INF model and eliminate the SNF missiles on a world-wide instead of only on a European basis. Such negotiations, if and when they begin, would obviously have a major impact on German-American security arrangements and consultations.

With all these negotiations either in train or expected to take place in the foreseeable future, arms control has acquired a life of its own. But arms control has several separate purposes, not all of which are compatible:

- To convey a political message to a potential opponent, theoretically inspiring confidence, an improvement in relations, and a reduction in mutual threat.
- To reduce the costs of military manpower, equipment, administration and deployment.
- To gain popularity at home and (in Gorbachev's case) abroad.
- To enhance security.

The latter purpose should theoretically dominate all considerations. It is the final standard against which all negotiations must be evaluated if the results are to endure. But in the current and prospective rounds of negotiations it will represent a difficult standard to meet because each negotiation must not only be evaluated on its own merits but also in terms of the effect that it has in combination with others. This is the main reason the United States has linked the conventional and SNF negotiations.

But the standard that prevails all too often in determining the direction and the priorities of arms control is that of popular appeal. Proposals and results are often judged not primarily for their strategic value but for their political potential. When Gorbachev promises reductions, Western leaders must match him even before he actually abolishes Soviet superiority or ceases the build-up of Soviet forces.

Allies often compete instead of collaborate in the popular aspect of arms control. A German author complained that the United States could not hope to bask in the aura of successive arms control treaties with the Soviet Union while asking the Europeans to bear the onus of installing new nuclear weapons systems.[25] No nation wants to appear to lag in its efforts. If the United States makes progress in START talks, Germany and other NATO states will want to move ahead in CFE and perhaps SNF.

Arms control priorities can and do conflict. The basic imbalance between East and West is in conventional strength. American nuclear power entered the European balance to match the massive presence of the Red Army. Therefore, the conventional balance must be set right as part of any total arms control accord. Conventional cuts would also save the most money and would most dramatically reduce the potential threat of war in Europe. But the popular outcry in the West is not for conventional but for nuclear reductions.

The disaffection of Western public opinion for the nuclear instrument began already in the 1960s when the United States believed that it had lost strategic superiority and introduced "flexible response."[26] It deepened throughout the 1970s and 1980s, because of encouragement through the Neutron Bomb, Reykjavik, anti-nuclear demonstrations, consistent Soviet exhortation, and genuine fear aroused by incidents like the nuclear accident at Chernobyl. By now, the nuclear deterrent has become virtually de-legitimized in the state that is most exposed to Soviet conventional power and that thus has the greatest interest in having the nuclear deterrent prevent war. But denuclearization has not happened only in Germany. American popular opposition to nuclear reactors and to deployment of the MX missile indicates that even in the United States there is widespread concern about nuclear accidents and about missiles as potential targets.

The arms control process can also revive the basic distinction between American and German perceptions on arms control treaties. Americans still see such treaties primarily as legal and security instruments. Germans, like many other continental Europeans, see arms control accords as political instruments that create a framework of confidence going beyond the texts of the accords themselves. That was the main reason the Federal Republic supported and even pushed the INF accord at the political level, whatever reservations some Germans may have had about some of its strategic aspects.

All these considerations must be brought into balance in order to be able to claim that Europe, the Federal Republic, and the United States are more secure at the end of the decade of arms control than they were at the beginning.

But Bonn and Washington have not yet agreed on the path to follow through the labyrinth of negotiations that lies ahead, and they have not found a balance between the values that they respectively attach to diplomatic and military security.

Future NATO Strategy
and German-American Ties

NATO and German-American strategic consultations since Gorbachev's arrival on the scene have often been single-issue-oriented, driven by urgent domestic political considerations or dramatic Soviet announcements, and heavily focused on prospective public pronouncements rather than alliance strategy.

NATO members have generally assumed that arms control consultations and negotiations would not alter basic strategic structures or conditions. They appear to have assumed that their strategy would remain intact. These assumptions have already proven wrong, and will certainly prove even more incorrect as arms control negotiations advance.

Basic NATO strategy, as formulated in the 1950s and modified in the 1960s, gave the Federal Republic of Germany the main conventional burden. It gave the United States the main burden of nuclear deterrence and a conventional role that would help couple Europe and America and would help defend West Germany. The main object was war prevention, and the main instrument was a chain of deterrence reaching from the single soldier on the West German front line to the U.S. Strategic Air Command in Omaha, Nebraska.

By 1989, however, with arms control discussions covering virtually every element of the NATO and Warsaw Pact arsenals, it was clear that arms control had become a vital part of strategy itself. It could no longer exist in a vacuum or focused on any single weapons system, but it had to march in tandem with the most basic concepts on how a war might be deterred or fought. Moreover, all Western consultation had to give due consideration to arms control as an aspect of strategy that could either weaken or reinforce NATO security.

At the same time, NATO was also reconsidering other aspects of its strategy because of political and technological changes. Thus, the discussion about strategy, arms control, modernization, self-deterrence, and singularization, had to take account of many prospects and proposals for political or strategic options:

- With respect to NATO itself, there have been proposals for the establishment of European security structures that would represent the common European interests in NATO and would enable the United States to ease its burdens while giving the European NATO publics—especially in West Germany—a sense of greater participation in NATO decision processes.[27]
- Several German analysts and political figures have urged a completely new NATO concept of "defensive defense," relying upon different military organizations and entirely new tactics, essentially abandoning forward defense.[28]
- Rapid changes in military technology, especially those arising out of powerful new conventional weapons, may compel a wholly new analysis of defense and deterrence requirements.
- New technologies and rules for monitoring compliance with arms control treaties may make it possible to maintain defense and deterrence at lower levels of expenditure but with equally stable results. New combinations of diplomatic and military security arrangements may emerge.

Ultimately, the object must be to provide greater assurance on all sides that states and nations are not under threat, and that they have enough time to prepare themselves if conditions should change. This requires clear understanding, especially within the NATO alliance, of what needs to be done on a continuing and on a contingency basis.

Bonn has for several years proposed a study for a NATO comprehensive concept *(Gesamptkonzept)*, searching for a system that would link diplomatic and military security and that would stabilize West Germany's situation. That concept did not emerge at the NATO 40th anniversary summit, even after a long period of preliminary consultation. All that did emerge was a concept paper for arms control.

The need for a strategic consensus has not been addressed, either within or outside NATO, within the United States or the Federal Republic, although the global strategic situation has evolved enough to raise some basic questions about the direction of Western security policy and about the extended deterrence principle that lies at its heart. American talk of SDI and of modernization, as well as German complaints about "singularization" and military overflights, do not reflect routine alliance bickering but broad strategic uncertainty and questioning.

If alliance consensus cannot be reached, there could be a crisis of strategy and of confidence. The United States and the Federal Republic would face special difficulties in such a situation. Past arrangements have been designed to meet their security needs as much as those of any other NATO partner. But at present neither can be certain that they can still coordinate as they should to maintain their mutual interests and obligations, and they now do not even articulate persuasively to their own electorates what those mutual interests and obligations are.

Among the questions that need to be answered, by Germans and Americans as well as other NATO members, are the following:

- Can extended deterrence, as conceived and implemented, still work under the new political pressures and potentially shifting military arrangements?
- Without extended deterrence, how is forward defense to operate under various potential new scenarios?
- If the current NATO strategy is no longer accepted by all NATO states and their people, what strategy will stabilize the European situation as well as extended deterrence and forward defense did for forty years?
- How must NATO now begin to prepare itself for a potentially different situation?
- If the European situation is going to shift substantially, with a different strategy and new balances emerging, what should be the U.S. military presence in and near Western Europe to match the

Soviets for the long haul and also to provide for the contingency of Soviet policy reversals?

• If the American role is reduced, how can the Federal Republic protect itself without disturbing others?

These are questions for NATO as a whole, but they are in the first instance questions for the United States and the Federal Republic.

Notes

1. A summary discussion of the process leading to the INF deployment is in David N. Schwarz, *NATO's Nuclear Dilemmas* (Washington: Brookings, 1983). Statistics on weapons deployment are drawn from appropriate annual publications of the International Institute for Strategic Studies, either *The Military Balance* or *Strategic Survey*.

2. Lewis Dunn, "Considerations after the INF Treaty," *Survival*, May/June 1988, pp. 195–198.

3. *The Economist*, May 6, 1989, p. 48.

4. For background, see *New York Times*, July 25, 1987.

5. Heinrich Fauth, "Die Tuecken des Nullsummen-Spiels," *Europaeische Wehrkunde*, May, 1987, pp. 254–256.

6. Wolfgang Ischinger, "Jenseits der Abschreckung," *Europa-Archiv*, June 22, 1988, pp. 342–343, summarizes German views.

7. Karl-Heinz Kamp, "Die Modernisierung der nuklearen Kurzstreckenwaffen in Europa," *Europa-Archiv*, May 25, 1988, pp. 269–276; *New York Times*, August 11, 1988.

8. *Financial Times*, February 10, 1989.

9. For background, see *New York Times*, February 13 and May 14, 1989.

10. As in Alfred Dregger interview in *Die Welt*, April 26, 1989.

11. *Frankfurter Allgemeine*, April 28 and June 23, 1988.

12. *New York Times*, February 17, 1989.

13. For background on options and issues, see Kamp, "Die Modernisierung," pp. 270–273; *New York Times*, August 11, 1988; *Washington Times*, September 22, 1988.

14. *Frankfurter Allgemeine*, April 25, 1989.

15. *Washington Post*, April 25, 1989.

16. "Deutschland-Nachrichten," April 26, 1989.

17. Summaries of the NATO proposals are in *Frankfurter Allgemeine*, May 30 and 31, 1989, and in *New York Times*, May 31 and June 4, 1989. The official NATO report is NATO Press Communique M-1(89)21, May 30, 1989.

18. President George Bush, "Proposal for a Free and Peaceful Europe," U.S. Department of State, Current Policy Paper No. 1179.

19. *Neue Zuercher Zeitung*, April 29/30, 1989.

20. *FBIS, Western Europe*, June 2, 1989.

21. Robert Blackwill, "Specific Approaches to Conventional Arms Control in Europe," *Survival*, September/October, 1988, pp. 43–44.

22. *Washington Post*, January 28, 1989.

23. *The German Tribune*, April 3, 1989.

24. *Frankfurter Allgemeine*, March 9 and 18, 1989.

25. Ischinger, "Jenseits der Abschreckung," p. 340.

26. Although, according to strategist Edward Luttwak, this was not then necessary because U.S. superiority was higher than before or since. See Edward Luttwak, "The Logic of Strategy and the Upkeep of Extended Deterrence," *Adelphi Papers*, Spring, 1989, p. 42.

27. Werner Weidenfeld, "Neuorganisation der Sicherheit Westeuropas," *Europa-Archiv*, May 10, 1987, p. 265.

28. These proposals are outlined by Anne-Marie LeGloannec, "West German Security: Less of a Consensus?" Catherine M. Kelleher and Gale Mattox, eds., *Evolving European Defense Policies* (Lexington, Mass.: D.C. Heath, 1987), pp. 169–184.

6

Relations with the East

Prussia, Germany, and Russia

The Costa Liguria, west of Genoa, is famous for its string of shining resorts reflected in the blue-green waters of the Mediterranean Sea. But one of those resorts, Rapallo, has become famous not only for its hotels and beaches but also for its place in European and world history. There, on Sunday, April 16, 1922, the delegations of republican Germany and of the communist Soviet Union met to sign the treaty now symbolic of a perennial Western fear—the Rapallo complex—that one day Germany will again turn its face toward the East and re-link its fate with Russia's.

That fear of a German turn to the East has reawakened, especially in the face of Gorbachev's dynamic diplomacy. The United States, as West Germany's principal security partner, cannot help but wonder what German-Soviet collaboration could mean for the security of Europe, for its own interests, and for the solidity of the German-American relationship.

Germans and Russians have a long history of contact, cooperation, competition, conflict, and reconciliation. That history goes back to medieval times, to encounters between the Holy Roman Empire and the Duchy of Muscovy, and to commerce and conflict between the settlements of the Teutonic Knights and the Russians attempting to reach toward the Baltic Sea. After the creation of the modern European state system, cycles of friendship and hostility intensified. Russia conquered and briefly occupied Frederick the Great's Berlin in 1759, a good 200 years before Khrushchev's Berlin ultimatum and the Wall. Prussia, Russia and Austria three times partitioned Poland as Prussia advanced east and Russia west. At Tauroggen and Kalisch, Prussia abandoned Napoleon after his return from Moscow and joined Alexander I in the alliance that helped to defeat the French Emperor and that gave Berlin a new weight in international diplomacy at the Congress of Vienna in 1814 and 1815. At various points in Russian history,

Germans helped to build Russian industry, Russian railroads, and the Russian navy.

After the German Empire became a major power in the wake of Prussia's defeat of France in 1870–1871, the German and Russian emperors exchanged regular correspondence although Berlin owed its closest loyalty to Russia's rival, Austria-Hungary. Germany's Chancellor Prince Otto von Bismarck preserved a secret relationship with St. Petersburg within the structure of the *Dreikaiserbund* of 1881 and through the Reinsurance Treaty of 1887 in order to keep Russia from moving closer to France. Kaiser Wilhelm II found the obligations of the Reinsurance Treaty legally and morally incompatible with Germany's fraternal links to Austria. He broke the Russian connection and thus opened the door to the Franco-Russian alliance that helped doom Germany in World War I.

Rapallo marked yet another try for post-imperial Germany and Russia. It provided the framework for a military and economic collaboration that was essential to both states at a time when they were the pariahs of world diplomacy. Berlin and Moscow chose to renew the treaty in 1926 although Germany under Gustav Stresemann was then reconciled with the West and the Soviet Union was more widely accepted than four years earlier (but still not recognized by Washington).

The Berlin-Moscow link continued, with variations, through the Hitler years. It helped to train and develop the *Wehrmacht*. It culminated in the Hitler-Stalin Pact that divided Eastern Europe and triggered World War II. Moscow, like St. Petersburg fifty years earlier, would have been prepared to continue its German tie in 1941. But Hitler attacked the Soviet Union, opening a cruel and bitter campaign that brought German troops to the gates of Moscow and Leningrad, that killed tens of millions of German and Russian soldiers and civilians, and that ultimately was to destroy Prussia and divide its capital while bringing Russia's borders and troops further than ever into the center of Europe.

There may be many lessons to draw for both nations from the history of the German-Russian relationship, but the most important are so evident and fundamental that they remain pertinent even at a time of intimate German-American relations: Germany and Russia cannot ignore each other, no matter what may be happening in the world, and both have usually done better when they cooperated than when they fought.

Germany's long history with the East does not consist only of its relations with the Russians but with all the nations of the area that used to be known as Central, Balkan, or Southeastern Europe, but that is now most often called Eastern Europe. Prussia and Germany at one time or another were friends or enemies with virtually all those peoples. Most of the nations were either with or against Germany in both world wars and in many earlier military or diplomatic campaigns. They have also had commercial and financial links with Germany for centuries, and have maintained diplomatic relations most of the time when they were independent.

The aristocrats of Russia and of Central and Eastern Europe mingled with Prussia's or Germany's in the salons and spas of Europe before World War I. Their people traveled to the great German cities for business or pleasure, having done it for centuries before the Iron Curtain and doing it again now. Germans have traveled there in turn. Their political parties have, whenever possible, maintained regular contacts with like-minded German parties to the present day. Although many European powers, such as the French, British, Austrians, or Italians, maneuvered in Eastern and Central Europe, the people of that area have always had a special interest and concern about all things German. Germans in turn always regarded that part of Europe with particular interest and even fascination. Their interest has grown all the more since World War II because part of what is termed Eastern Europe, or of the Soviet sphere, used to be part of Germany itself.

The United States has no comparable set of relationships. Except for brief times when Russian actions or developments required special notice, as in early competition along the Pacific rim, the purchase of Alaska, or the Russian Revolution and its aftermath, the United States before World War II rarely considered Russia or the Soviet Union to be important to its own interests. Americans had strong links to some Central European nations, especially the Poles, but those were founded at least as much on the East European origins of millions of U.S. citizens and voters as on foreign policy considerations.

After World War II, U.S. attitudes toward Eastern Europe were heavily influenced by large numbers of refugees that fled Eastern Europe either before or during the Stalinist period. The refugees vividly recalled and recounted the horrors of the communist conquest of their countries. The United States felt alternately guilty or frustrated that it had even made the Yalta agreements or that it had not been able to enforce them in such a way that the countries of the region could have enjoyed freedom.

In approaching the Soviet Union and Eastern Europe, therefore, the Federal Republic and the United States start from different historical, geographical, political, and economic foundations and premises. Those differences carried little weight when the strategic and political interests of both countries mandated a strong and united defense against the

Soviet and satellite armies. But they emerge strongly when the threat appears to subside, whether temporarily or permanently.

It is little wonder, therefore, that policy toward the East can generate confusion and mistrust in German-American ties. Yet some of the most important aspects of German-American relations must be played out in this area, especially as Gorbachev advances his proposals for new political and economic structures, as the entire European continent continues to evolve, and as West Germany again senses a potential for genuine influence toward the East.

German-American Coordination in the Cold War and Detente

The time when Germany and America had separate interests toward the Soviet Union and Eastern Europe ended abruptly in 1945, when the United States in effect became a European power. From the founding of the Federal Republic until now, Washington and Bonn have constantly had to coordinate their policies toward Moscow and Eastern Europe or at least to be aware of the activities of the other. That coordination, and occasional lack of coordination, has become a sensitive topic between Washington and Bonn.

Coordination proved relatively uncomplicated in the 1940s and 1950s because the United States, as one of the victors, pursued the policies it needed or wished in Germany and found willing supporters there. As it became clear after 1945 that no peace treaty could be immediately negotiated, that a Soviet presence meant Stalinism, and that most Germans in the Western occupation zones preferred to cast their lot with the West, the United States and the new West German government shared common interests and attitudes. Although Chancellor Adenauer in 1955 visited Moscow to conclude an agreement for mutual recognition and for the release of German prisoners, there was no divergence of basic West German and U.S. policies. The United States supported the new West German government in its application of the Hallstein doctrine which insisted that West Germany would not have relations with any government (except Moscow's) that recognized the GDR.

Bonn and Washington generally reinforced each other during the Berlin crisis of 1958–1962, but divergences appeared as the Germans were disturbed by some U.S. compromise proposals and by Washington's decision to accept the Berlin Wall without challenge. Rumors circulated in Berlin and West Germany that the United States had agreed in advance to the building of the Wall. Washington emphatically denied those rumors, which may have been instigated by Moscow to foment German-American mistrust. But it was widely known that

President Kennedy and his advisers did not believe that the old Chancellor had the imagination needed to negotiate with Moscow.

By 1966, with the formation of the government of Kurt Georg Kiesinger, different types of divergences appeared. The new Bonn government, and particularly the members of the SPD, favored early negotiations with Moscow to ease the effects of Germany's division. Although the United States had already proposed in 1963 that Bonn should talk to Moscow about the future of Germany, Washington still followed the contacts between Bonn and Moscow with some concern. It wanted no arrangement that would weaken the U.S. position in Berlin and Germany or that would give recognition to the GDR.

After Nixon had announced the "era of negotiations" and after a new West German government even more committed to *Ostpolitik* and detente had been formed under Brandt and Foreign Minister Walter Scheel in 1969, coordination of West German and American policies became a particularly important element for the success of negotiations with Moscow and East Berlin. Although Bonn's talks with the Soviet Union and the GDR were coordinated with general American detente negotiations and with the British and French governments, both Bonn and Washington had their doubts about the frankness and effectiveness of that coordination.

Much of the German-American coordination of detente negotiations was informal, running through a back channel message circuit between Nixon's and Brandt's advisers Kissinger and Bahr.[1] It was also absolutely essential. Moscow had the greater interest in its negotiations with Bonn and in the inter-German talks. It wanted West German recognition of the GDR, of the postwar borders, and of the advanced Soviet presence. The Western powers had the greater interest in the quadripartite negotiations on Berlin, where they wanted to arrange a regime not subject to constant Soviet/GDR chicanery. Bonn also wanted a more stable situation in Berlin. But coordination became very complicated because Washington was also negotiating with Moscow on strategic arms, with Beijing on re-establishing relations, and with Hanoi on a Vietnam peace arrangement, whereas Bonn was also talking with Warsaw and additionally often found itself in the difficult position of negotiating on issues that would normally have been part of a peace treaty to be agreed by and with all the victors.

German-American consultation had to consider both the timing and the substance of the various talks. The Soviet inclination to play its interlocutors against each other helped complicate that coordination, as did the perceived U.S. need for separate private and official channels. Only the greatest effort on all sides made the coordination succeed, despite its imperfections, but it still left a residue of suspicion on both the U.S. and the West German sides.[2] This was mitigated by their mutual satisfaction at having achieved agreements that helped stabilize the situation in Berlin, permitted greater contacts across the Wall, and broke the deadlock in Central Europe.

The detente agreements recognized a place for the United States in the center of Europe through the Quadripartite Agreement on Berlin and through the conditions that Brandt had placed on the talks (see below). The Helsinki agreements of 1975 reinforced the U.S. role in Europe. But American public opinion did not welcome this as much as it resented the recognition of a Soviet presence in Central Europe and especially the recognition of the East European borders and regimes. Conservative elements of the Republican Party, including Ronald Reagan, severely attacked President Gerald Ford for the Helsinki accords.

German and American perceptions of detente began to diverge after 1973 and even more after 1975, not only because of different assessments of the Helsinki results but also because Bonn and Washington faced very different situations. The agreements applicable to Berlin and Germany remained in place and were generally obeyed by all the concerned parties, giving Bonn and the West German public a benign view of relations with Moscow. On the other hand, the United States was acutely conscious of a Soviet global challenge that was not equally felt in Bonn.

Although the situation in Europe remained generally calm, Washington repeatedly had to counter a Soviet challenge to peace and to U.S. interests outside Europe. Brezhnev, increasingly weak and ultimately senile, could still maintain good relations with the West German government and could get a friendly reception in Bonn, but Washington found itself in a global confrontation and turned increasingly skeptical about relations with Moscow.

The Soviet decision to deploy the SS-20 missiles and the succession of aged and incapacitated Kremlin leaders offered more of a military than a diplomatic challenge to the West after 1977. Although Chancellor Schmidt believed that the administration of President Carter could have negotiated more effectively with Moscow about arms control, broad German and American perceptions about the prospects for success in East-West negotiations largely coincided again by the end of the decade. The NATO INF decision of 1979 and Moscow's refusal to negotiate led to another chill in East-West relations. Until the actual deployment of NATO INF weapons in 1983, Moscow singled out West Germany and the United States for special denunciation.

German-American differences diminished as East-West relations soured in the latter 1970s, but that amelioration was deceptive. Mutual collaboration and understanding of each other's respective needs and interests did not improve. Instead, there were very few diplomatic opportunities. Bonn and Washington had not found an effective way to work together in their dealings with the East, but had only been given a respite by Soviet immobilism. This quickly became obvious when a new leader in Moscow launched a rapid-fire cycle of European and arms control diplomacy.

Gorbachev, Reagan, and Kohl

German-American difficulties in coordinating their Eastern policies erupted after Gorbachev came to power and made it clear almost from the beginning that he wanted quickly to improve relations with the West. He met with President Reagan in 1985 in Geneva and then four more times before Reagan left office. The summits in Reykjavik, Moscow, and Washington dealt with subjects of great interest to the Federal Republic because they had a direct effect on the effectiveness of extended deterrence in NATO. Although Reagan and Gorbachev were negotiating about American and Soviet weapons systems, they were also negotiating about the strategic balance in Europe and therefore about German security. Bonn was bound to follow those talks with interest and some concern, a concern exaggerated by its own lack of strategic weapons and its dependence on the U.S. deterrent. Gorbachev's tactics did not ease Bonn's worries, as his handling of the Pershing IA showed that he believed major weapons systems were for great powers and not for others to decide.

But Gorbachev did not want to deal only with the United States. He wanted to end the totality of Soviet isolation. That meant dealing with Europe and with Bonn, although he handled relations with the Federal Republic in a distant and sometimes perplexing way. Soon after his accession, Gorbachev visited London and Paris, evoking generally positive responses in those capitals and considerable interest in German political and media circles. But he did not visit Bonn and he at first showed little interest in doing so. There were suggestions that he was anti-German because he had as a child experienced Nazi occupation. Gorbachev may also have been disappointed because Kohl supported SDI even after Gorbachev had personally appealed to him not to do so.

Whatever the reasons, Gorbachev did not visit Bonn or invite Kohl to Moscow. He and other Soviet officials invited a host of other German officials, including President Richard von Weizsaecker, Genscher, Strauss and many members of the opposition. Some of the early invitations may have represented a deliberate snub toward Kohl, who retaliated by stating that Gorbachev, like Goebbels, was an excellent propagandist but that he had to take some concrete actions before his policies could be evaluated. That remark could not have pleased Gorbachev, and may have further complicated relations.

In a broader sense, Gorbachev may not yet have been certain about how to fit the Federal Republic into his global diplomatic plans. He had begun with the United States, Great Britain, and France, which were nuclear powers. The Federal Republic had no nuclear weapons, but it could not be ignored because of its conventional forces and its wealth. Thus, Gorbachev may well have decided to turn to Bonn only after he had made some preliminary efforts with others and had perceived more clearly what he needed in Central Europe.

The German-Soviet standoff was not broken until October 1988, when Kohl visited Moscow on a formal invitation from Gorbachev, with Gorbachev promising to pay a return visit to Bonn in June 1989. The double visit arrangement was based on a compromise. Kohl did not wish to visit Moscow first because he had been there several times for funerals and Gorbachev had taken the initiative to visit several other Western capitals. But Gorbachev said that he would not go to Bonn until Kohl had come to Moscow. The Germans therefore considered the two visits as one entity, to be announced simultaneously, and with no document to be issued until after the second. The Soviets, who did not want to delay the meetings any further, agreed.

Kohl's visit to Moscow was not free of strain.[3] He did not develop the kind of warm relationship that Reagan and others had developed with Gorbachev. The visit was stiff, somewhat cold, but correct, in the words of German officials. Nonetheless, the visit was significant in terms of what it accomplished and the openings that it offered to both countries, especially as Kohl and Gorbachev had five hours of private conversation.

Kohl used his principal speech in Moscow to reiterate the German desire for reunification and to state that any progress in German-Soviet relations had to include Berlin.[4] Kohl said that Germans respected existing borders and would only seek reunification by peaceful means, but that no amount of polemicizing would alter the fact that the division of the country was "unnatural." Gorbachev down-played these problems by replying that the "so-called German question" was "a product of history," and that any effort to alter the reality would represent an "incalculable and even dangerous undertaking."[5] As for Berlin, he said that Moscow would accept West Berlin's inclusion in European and international agreements but that the city's "special status" remained unalterable.

Gorbachev spoke of the Soviet Union and the Federal Republic as members of a "common European home," but he observed that Moscow recognized West Germany's links to other countries and the obligations it had assumed. In obvious reference to NATO consultations on short-range missile modernization, he warned that agreements such as the INF treaty should not be undermined.

Gorbachev concentrated major portions of his statement on economic relations. He asserted that Soviet "restructuring" *(perestroika)* would succeed and that it offered enormous potential. He stated that the Soviet Union would "extend its faithful hand" to those who were prepared to participate, hinting that German economic cooperation might pay off in political relations.

Kohl, like his host, spoke of the potential for economic cooperation, recalling that the Federal Republic was the Soviet Union's most important Western trading partner and citing German readiness to work with the Soviet Union "in new forms of cooperation." As for the "common European home," Kohl insisted that any European system had to include links to the "North American democracies." He also asked Gorbachev to reduce the considerable Soviet advantage in short-range missiles, but received no answer. In his statement to the press at the conclusion of his visit to Moscow, Kohl reiterated his interest in German unity and added that "for us, the last word of history has not been spoken."[6] Kohl's aides pointed out separately that Kohl had not raised the issue of German reunification because he expected a positive response but because he wished to explore and clarify the extent of Gorbachev's readiness to change the fundamental situation in Europe.

What Kohl's visit to Moscow may have lacked in warmth, it compensated in substance. The German and Soviet government and banking officials signed a large number of agreements for cooperation in economic and financial areas. Chief among the accords was a thirteen-year loan of DM 3 billion ($1.7 billion) to help re-equip Soviet light industry, one of Gorbachev's top priorities.[7] The loans were tied to the actual purchase of equipment, not credits to be used for any purpose. A number of other accords were also signed, governing cooperation in environmental, cultural, technical and commercial areas. Some of the more significant accords involved nuclear industrial cooperation, including a contract for German firms to construct a DM 1 billion high temperature nuclear reactor in the Soviet Union.

The Moscow agreements promised the Soviet Union a share in advanced Western technology that had frequently been denied by the West and whose sale to the Soviet Union had initially been opposed by the United States, although there were indications that these particular contracts had been informally discussed with U.S. officials and that the United Sates would raise no objection.[8] Nonetheless, some of the German credits and contacts were greeted in the American press as evidence of an eastward drift in Bonn's policies, with charges that the Federal Republic had secretly guaranteed the loans and had made special deals regarding technology transfer.[9]

Gorbachev in Bonn

Gorbachev's return visit to the Federal Republic from June 12 to 15, 1989, was a triumph of "Gorbomania" but also contained important substantive elements. The schedule had to be curtailed because problems in the Soviet Union would compel Gorbachev to remain in the Soviet embassy several hours every day for telephone calls to Moscow, but it still allowed ample time for public demonstrations, for Gorbachev's patented mingling with crowds, and for substantive discussions. To underline his interest in the economic and commercial aspects of German-Soviet relations, Gorbachev went to the centers of German industry in Duesseldorf and Stuttgart as well as to his political meetings in Bonn.[10]

Gorbachev again showed himself a master of the politics of promise. He made speeches that told the West Germans what they wanted to hear, and reputedly took with him an expert on Germany whose task it was to give him specific advice on that subject. He did not speak of the past. Instead, he spoke of the future. He spoke of peace, of cooperation, and of the "common European home." He spoke in glowing terms of the promise of German-Soviet collaboration, especially in commercial and economic dealings. He visited West German factories and admired the latest in German technology. He hinted that Germany might not forever remain divided, and said that the Wall could come down when conditions had changed enough to permit it to happen. At his closing press conference, he said that "everything is possible."

Gorbachev also stressed peace and disarmament. He pledged reduction of conventional forces and also called for the elimination of short-range nuclear forces, putting additional pressure on the Western alliance for accommodation. He did not promise to abolish the short-range weapons world-wide, but spoke of their elimination only with respect to Europe. Ultimately, he said, no state should have forces on foreign territory.

Kohl and other Germans also spoke of peace and arms control but reminded Gorbachev of German problems. Kohl said that the division of Germany was "an open wound." Lothar Spaeth, the Minister-President of Baden-Wuerttemberg, said that no European home could be built with a Wall running through the middle.

The final declaration, a document that had taken a year and numerous interventions at senior levels to negotiate, reflected these differences in attitudes and objectives while laying out a broad basis for German-Soviet relations.[11] To the pleasure of the Germans, and at their insistence, it assigned a place to the United States and Canada in the "common European home" (also see below) and it arranged for the inclusion of West Berlin in the further development of cooperation between the Federal Republic and the Soviet Union. It spoke of the right of self-determination for every state to choose its own political and social system, a pledge that Bonn interpreted as formal renunciation of the Brezhnev doctrine. It also contained commitments to a Europe that would remain at peace, to the development of pan-European cooperation, and to a wide-ranging array of arms control agreements and negotiations that would produce "a stable balance at a lower level that will be adequate for defense but not for attack."

As part of the positive mood developed during the visit, Kohl and Gorbachev promised to maintain their personal contacts and there were reports that Kohl might again visit Moscow during 1990.

Prospects for German-Soviet Cooperation

Whatever political commitments may have been made by Bonn and Moscow, however, Gorbachev's visit made its greatest progress in German-Soviet economic cooperation. The two states committed themselves, before and during that visit, to steps that would give the Federal Republic a potentially vital role in the modernization of the Soviet economy.

Some of the principal elements of that cooperation, as agreed in Bonn or before, are the following:

• A growing list of joint ventures, already well over fifty at the time of Gorbachev's visit, ranging across a wide array of products with more to come.[12] Many of the agreed joint ventures are to be in consumer products, helping to fulfill an important element in Gorbachev's *perestroika* pledge and almost certainly giving him a chance for earlier success than Soviet industry could reach on its own. During Kohl's visit to Moscow, he was accompanied by fifty German businessmen, many of them exploring possible joint ventures in the Soviet Union although they were cautious because in the past few such ventures had made money.[13] Several of these businessmen were also present during Gorbachev's visit to Bonn.

Whatever its reservations, West German business led the world in joint ventures with the Soviet Union.[14] Gorbachev made a special appeal to German investors during his visit and signed an agreement for the protection of foreign investors.

- A Soviet agreement to purchase at least 300,000 Siemens personal computers, at a total price of DM 1.5 billion, to be reportedly used mainly by the Education Ministry and perhaps to be partly assembled in the Soviet Union.[15] The agreement, believed to be Moscow's largest ever purchase of foreign computers, could give German computer industry an important role in the future development of personal computers within the Soviet Union. It could also provide a valuable foundation of contact and collaboration for German industry in an area of growing importance where the Soviet Union clearly needs help and will continue to need it.
- A host of other accords signed in Bonn, eleven in all, which in their totality add up to significant economic cooperation, such as training of Soviet managers in West Germany and the building of a "house of the German economy" with offices and a hotel in the center of Moscow.[16]
- Long-run trade prospects which led the West German Economics Minister Helmut Haussmann to describe the Soviet Union as Germany's "ideal economic partner," a country where German goods could be sold after other markets of the world had reached their saturation point.[17]

The West German credit agreed during Kohl's visit to Moscow was only one of many credits being offered by Western governments, including Great Britain, Italy, and France. It was—at least on the surface—less generous than some of the other arrangements, especially because it was not guaranteed by the West German government. The guarantees were not necessary, as German bankers were generally willing to lend to the Soviet Union because Soviet credit has been good. At the time of Gorbachev's visit to Bonn, less than a year after the credit program was launched, one half of the credits had reportedly already been drawn.

German-Soviet commercial exchanges, especially Soviet exports, had declined since the early 1980s, largely because the decline of world energy prices had reduced Soviet capacity to earn foreign exchange. Both countries wanted to reverse the trend.[18] The German Economics Ministry reported that trade had improved in 1988 and that there were prospects for further improvement.[19]

German officials and businessmen often said that they supported trade and contacts with the Soviet Union because they believed that such steps would support Gorbachev's restructuring of the Soviet economy, expand liberalization of Soviet society, and in the long run make the Soviet Union more prosperous and less inclined to military ventures or pressures. They saw the advent of Russian consumerism and the opening of the political system as advantages for the West. Nonetheless, they persistently stressed that German trade with Moscow remained relatively small, below the level of German-Danish trade, largely because of Russia's incapacity to produce useful exports other than raw materials.[20]

German-Soviet economic contacts and exchanges agreed during 1988 and 1989 went beyond trade, however, offering Gorbachev significant support for the economic progress that he wished to accomplish. To that extent, they went into the realm of politics. They mixed the persistent German and Russian mutual interest with very practical economic benefits for both sides.

Although many other countries—including the United States—were disposed to cooperate economically with the Soviet Union, the steps that Bonn was taking would assist materially in the modernization of the Soviet economy and in whatever prospects for success Gorbachev's restructuring program might have.

With Germany's opening to Moscow came expanded German opportunities in Eastern Europe. Gorbachev's visit to Bonn sanctioned greater German commercial activities and influence in those countries, and senior Soviet officials were reported to believe that the German presence could encourage reforms and economic progress.[21] In that respect, the Federal Republic was developing in Eastern Europe, as well as in the Soviet Union, a presence and influence that Germany had not had since 1914, and that it could not have had without Soviet concurrence. German officials believed that Gorbachev's acceptance of the Bonn declaration, with its stress on self-determination, also sanctioned German encouragement of greater human rights and freedom in those countries.

Gorbachev's policies in 1988 and 1989, and particularly his visit to Bonn, endorsed *Ostpolitik* and even put a seal of approval upon it. Gorbachev had thus associated himself with a powerful tradition in German history, and also with growing German belief in the reestablishment of a pan-European environment in which the Federal Republic would have an important role to play. This combination, together with his apparent determination to ease the military confrontation in Central Europe, could not help but make him popular in Germany.

The "Common European Home" and "Genscherism"

One of the most striking images evoked by Gorbachev and other Soviet officials has been the concept of a "common European home from the Atlantic to the Urals," an image that he did not originate but has developed more extensively than any Soviet leader. Gorbachev has spoken of this on many occasions, including his meetings with Germans and his visit to Germany. He has plainly wanted to use it to appeal to Europeans by suggesting a community of nations living in neighborly peace and harmony on a common continent. Such an appeal finds fertile ground in West Germany as well as in other European countries at a time when the sense of a pan-European identity is spreading throughout Western and Eastern Europe. It cannot have the same attraction for the United States, as it also suggests that Moscow will have a voice in European events but Washington will not.

Russians and Germans discussed the "European home" before Kohl's visit to Moscow, during an informal 1987 Moscow meeting sponsored by the German Bergedorfer Gespraechskreis. When several Soviet officials at the meeting began sounding the theme, the German participants asked whether the United States was to be included in that home. The Soviets demurred, but the German participants persisted.[22] Several of them, including Ruehe and Bahr, said that the United States and Canada had to be part of the "European home."[23] Soviet officials opposed it. Valentin Falin, former Soviet Ambassador to Bonn, said that the United States was seeking a "special role" in Europe as an "administrator," a role that he unequivocally rejected. He said to the Germans that they had to choose between the new "European home" and the home in which they were, suggesting that Gorbachev's concept was incompatible with West Germany's current treaty arrangements with the United States and others.[24] When Ruehe said that the Soviet Union was also a non-European power, the head of the Soviet Institute for the United States and Canada, Georgi Arbatov, accused him of "polemics."[25] One Soviet representative said that the Soviet Union was "not against" the concept of an independent European defense system, an invitation for the Europeans to withdraw from NATO and extended deterrence.[26] The meeting ended in a stand-off on the subject.

In December, 1988, a second meeting of the same Bergedorfer Gespraechskreis took place in Bonn, but with a strikingly different result. At that meeting, Soviet officials said that an American role in Europe would be not only possible but necessary. The Soviet statements, made by Central Committee member Vadim Zagladin and others, constituted Moscow's strongest endorsement to that date for a U.S. presence in the "European home."[27] Privately, Soviet officials told German conference participants even more firmly that they favored an American presence. Gorbachev himself later officially endorsed the American and Canadian place in a "common European home" in the Bonn declaration.

West Germans officials and others were pleased at the outcome of the "common European home" debate with Moscow, concluding that their earlier statements and Kohl's insistence during his visit to Moscow had helped persuade the Soviets to review their position. Some believed that earlier Soviet statements had been a trial balloon to drive a wedge between Bonn and Washington, and they were satisfied that they had been able to correct both the public record as well as Soviet perceptions about German attitudes.

Whatever the reason for Moscow's shift, it eased at least one possible source of German-American friction over West Germany's relations to Moscow. It suggested that Gorbachev would be prepared to pay attention to German views on the political and security structure of Europe even if he was not prepared to envisage Germany as a partner in global strategic discussions. It also indicated, however, that Moscow still could not resist the temptation to generate German-American friction when an occasion presented itself.

Another cause of confusion and tension in German-American relations was American concern about what came to be called "Genscherism," a term U.S. officials and journalists used to describe what they perceived as the exaggerated desire of the West German Foreign Minister for accommodation with Moscow—if necessary at the expense of American and perhaps even West German security interests. American officials and others expressed the fear that Genscher was so eager to make concessions to Moscow that he would agree to denuclearize NATO and to make arrangements that would leave only a tattered and ineffectual U.S. presence in Europe.[28]

The U.S. impression was based in part on statements that Genscher made on various visits to Moscow but even more on several speeches he made. In the first, delivered to the World Economic Forum in Davos, Switzerland, on February 1, 1987, Genscher (in the official English translation) said that Gorbachev had to be "taken at his word" and that there was a common and mutual East-West interest in security.[29] Although he warned that the West was still only faced with "a possibility" of a new Soviet policy and had to sustain its strength, he vigorously advocated taking advantage of the opportunity to shape a new international security environment, especially in Europe.

Genscher followed a similar line in speeches to an international conference at Potsdam and at the Johns Hopkins University Bologna Center in June and October 1988.[30] In the Potsdam speech, he recalled his own childhood in East Germany and spoke of the need for closer

East-West ties. He down-played the American role in Europe but pleaded for a forthcoming Western attitude toward Gorbachev. He did not repeat that the West should "take Gorbachev at his word" but said that it should "hold him to his word," and he added that the West should help Gorbachev's efforts to restructure the Soviet Union. He appeared to call for Western support of the Soviet Union and for positive Western responses to Soviet proposals. He also spoke in highly positive terms about a "common European home" and about the future of Europe, adding to the impression that he minimized the American and trans-Atlantic connection as well as the military requirements of the Western security structure.

Genscher may have spoken with a political purpose toward German domestic opinion and toward Moscow at a time when Kohl had not yet visited Moscow and when German-Soviet relations were in the process of transformation. He may have been trying to adjust to growing "Gorbomania" in German opinion. Although Kohl had consistently stated that Germany had to judge Gorbachev on the basis of what he did, not of what he said, a number of Americans were disturbed by Genscher's remarks. They put them together with Bonn's advancing *Ostpolitik,* often run directly out of Genscher's office, and concluded that Genscher was engaged in a process dangerous to the NATO alliance and to U.S. interests.

To help ease U.S. concerns, Genscher's subsequent speeches stressed the important U.S. role as a partner for Europe.[31] Otto Graf Lambsdorff, chairman of the FDP, used a Washington visit in February 1989 to reiterate that Genscher did not mean that Gorbachev should be "taken at his word" but that he should be "held to his word." Lambsdorff said that Genscher's position was no different from the U.S. view, frequently articulated by Reagan as "trust, but verify".[32] Even after Lambsdorff's efforts, U.S. officials again raised the specter of "Genscherism" when the Federal Republic proposed arms control talks about short-range nuclear weapons. Nonetheless, after a special visit by Genscher to Washington in June 1989 to brief the U.S. government on the Gorbachev visit to Bonn, U.S. officials pronounced themselves reassured about "Genscherism" and about the constancy of West German policy.[33] Genscher himself said that President Bush had expressed no concern about excessive West German accommodation toward Moscow.[34]

The "European home" and "Genscherism" discussions underlined the sensitivity just below the surface of German-American relations about any German negotiations with Moscow, and the opportunities for misunderstanding and mutual suspicion that quickly arise.

The two discussions also demonstrated the difficulties that the Federal Republic faced. German officials and others had to make the Soviets understand that Germany would not participate in a European home without the United States. On the other hand, they had to make U.S. officials understand that they would say things that sounded troublesome to American ears but that were not intended to dissolve the German-American link. The new world of diplomatic security might be tempting, but it would not always be easy for the Germans or for their companions.

Inter-German Relations

Relations between the two states in the German nation, East and West Germany, are one of the most important elements of German policy toward the East, although the West German government sees them as separate because they represent inter-German, not foreign, relations. They are an area for German concentration, with a much lower degree of U.S. involvement, but there is a separate and important U.S. interest. Beyond this, they are also potentially part of any envisaged restructuring of Europe.

The immediate West German interest in relations with East Germany is, above all else, humanitarian. Many West Germans feel privileged and secure in the Federal Republic but are acutely aware of the lower levels of political freedom and of well-being in the GDR. Many have relatives there. West Germans see East Germany as part of the same nation and most want to do everything possible not to lose contact. Many also want to promote political liberties and economic progress in the GDR. This is one of the important reasons for inter-German trade, which offers the GDR opportunities for access to the European Community market to such a degree that the GDR is sometimes described as the Community's thirteenth member.

The U.S. interest is, in immediate terms, much more limited, but it is significant in the legal issues surrounding the German problem. It arises out of the residual U.S. responsibility for all of Germany as one of the victorious powers of World War II. In the absence of a peace settlement, the United States—like the Soviet Union, France, and Great Britain—retains a certain authority and responsibility. Some U.S. responsibilities, like those in the air corridors to Berlin or those of the U.S. Military Mission to the Soviet commander in East Germany, are exercised every day. Others are not exercised at all.

Bonn and Washington have always agreed that it was important to maintain U.S. residual authority and rights, and they have also agreed that nothing in inter-German relations should disturb U.S. and NATO defense arrangements in Europe. The Soviets have also preserved their residual rights in East Germany, even more conscientiously than the Western victors in West Germany, and have an important defense interest in East Germany.

Ever since inter-German negotiations began as part of the German detente process in 1970, West German authorities have made certain that U.S. and other allied rights would be kept separate from the negotiations. This was evident in the inter-German negotiations during the time of detente in the early 1970s and it is equally evident during recent contacts between West and East Germany. Nonetheless, the very fact that these talks take place means that the Federal Republic is negotiating substantively if indirectly about the situation in Germany with one of the victorious powers, the Soviet Union. To compensate for this, the Federal Republic must be constantly alert that it is representing the interests of the Western powers as well as its own, and there are frequent consultations in Bonn to avoid any misunderstanding

When Chancellor Brandt opened the door to inter-German talks in his speech before the West German *Bundestag* on January 14, 1970, his statement showed that the Chancellor understood Allied and American concerns in the discussions that were to follow.[35] He said that the Paris Treaties (establishing West German participation in NATO) were not a subject for negotiation, and that the existing rights and responsibilities of the four powers with regard to Germany as a whole and to Berlin were to be respected. He added that both East and West Germany were obligated to maintain the unity of the German nation.

Four months later, during Brandt's second meeting with GDR Prime Minister Willy Stoph, Brandt stressed an additional point that was also an American as well as West German interest: The links that had developed between West Berlin and West Germany were to be maintained and respected.[36] The Western allied ambassadors made a similar statement to the Soviet ambassador.

When the inter-German talks were concluded with an agreement between Bonn and the GDR, the United States and other allies approved. Later, the United States established diplomatic relations with East Germany.

Relations between the Germanies since then have had a life of their own. They have been largely insulated from East-West tensions, not only during the global breakdown of detente after 1973 but even when the Soviet Union broke off the arms control talks and denounced the Federal Republic along with the entire West during the NATO INF deployment. The two German states continued to make some progress in their bilateral relations despite global or European tensions. Even the advent of the government of Helmut Kohl, whose CDU/CSU had opposed the inter-German accords, did not disrupt ties. Kohl in office has sought further improvement in inter-German contacts.

The most notable sign of progress has been in personal travel. More than 2 million West German visits to the GDR have taken place every year during the 1980s. In return, there have annually been at least 1.5 million visits of pensioners from East to West. From 1981 through 1985, there were between 50,000 and 65,000 visits to West Germany and West Berlin each year by East Germans and East Berliners below pension age traveling for urgent family reasons.[37] In 1986, the latter number suddenly jumped to almost 600,000, a remarkable nine-fold increase.[38] It increased to over 1.2 million in 1987, and to 3 million in 1988. Added to the number of pensioners, a total of over 5 million East German visits to West Germany took place during 1988. Kohl has pointed to this figure with satisfaction.[39] In March 1989 the GDR eased travel regulations, making it easier for persons from the GDR to travel to the West.[40] The move was welcomed in West Germany.

Relatively few of the travelers from East Germany from 1985 through 1988 remained in the West, which may have increased East German confidence that they could be permitted to travel in greater numbers. Most of them, as in the past, still had to leave family members at home. And refugees from the GDR continue to come to West Germany. In 1988, there were almost 10,000, the highest total since 1965.[41]

Further steps to ease the burdens of the division of Germany also occurred during 1988, from agreements that have made travel arrangements easier—and which have permitted unprecedented appeals when travel permits are denied—to agreements on youth travel and city-to-city links.[42] However, Kohl and other West German officials have complained that the GDR authorities have not introduced some of the political liberalization measures that Gorbachev has introduced in the Soviet Union under *glasnost*. In fact, the GDR has resisted introduction of such measures and has indicated that it plans to maintain its political and economic system as well as its current leadership. It has even restricted circulation of Soviet publications inside East Germany, including the Soviet magazine *Sputnik* that printed articles attacking Stalin and the magazine *Novoye Vremya* when it printed an interview with Polish "Solidarity" leader Lech Walesa.[43] The GDR has, however, matched Gorbachev's announcement of unilateral troop reductions by announcing its own prospective cut of 10,000.

A pattern of positive and negative developments prevails as inter-German relations continue. Although public opinion and political figures in West Germany were pleased over improved travel arrangements, they were very disturbed at the beginning of 1989 when shootings and other incidents at the Wall again called attention to East German violations of human rights. West German officials cancelled visits to the GDR.[44] The GDR pledged to "humanize" the border regime, but incidents offensive to West German and American public opinion have continued to occur.

As an additional spur to closer relations, former East German chief of state Erich Honecker visited West Germany in September 1987. Such a visit had been planned twice before, in 1984 and 1985, but cancelled at Moscow's insistence, first to protest West German stationing of the INF missiles and later because of Soviet concern that inter-German relations were becoming too intimate.

Honecker's visit to West Germany concentrated for the most part on the familiar inter-German agenda.[45] He and his West German hosts signed an environmental agreement as well as agreements on science and technology and on cooperation against hazardous radiation. He also visited his homeland in the Saar. Although his visit was only labeled as "official," the West Germans treated it almost like a state visit. Flags were flown and anthems played, and Honecker called on all senior West German officials.

Honecker spoke repeatedly of the importance of good East-West relations, especially arms control and measures to improve security in Europe. Several times, he linked progress on inter-German relations with the overall East-West dialogue, which implied that Bonn should press the United States to improve the East-West climate and help inter-German relations. The joint communique at the end of the visit reinforced this link, with both Germanies committing themselves to using their influence within their respective alliances toward "relaxing tensions and ensuring peace."

Despite Honecker's plea, it appears unlikely that the agenda for inter-German talks would begin to concentrate on major East-West matters and would have an impact of Soviet-American negotiations. The technical, economic and environmental issues on the inter-German agenda are complicated enough, and they can prove stubborn and costly to resolve. There will also undoubtedly be further talks by which West Germany will attempt to improve travel, human rights, exchanges of persons, and other measures to ease the plight of families split between the two Germanies or the two halves of Berlin. This is an agenda that should provide enough material for progress in inter-German relations in directions that would not disturb the United States.

Over the longer run, the future of inter-German relations remains unclear. In an historical sense, East and West Germany are taking the first steps toward re-establishing elements of the Holy Roman Empire although without the Emperor. In that Empire, which largely covered the German-speaking peoples of Western and Central Europe, states of

German nationality were separated by political and by religious boundaries. But citizens of the Empire could travel from state to state within the Empire. They shared certain elements in common even if they were not in the same political or economic entity. They had a sense of a larger commonality even if that larger commonality did not affect their lives on a daily basis as much as their immediate political masters did.

If relations between the two Germanies continue to make progress, and if human as well as economic and cultural contacts continue to develop, what can emerge is a structure in which the elements of commonality, even if they do not prevail at the political level, begin to make a significant impact on the lives and the thinking of the citizens. It was this element of the Empire that began to generate a common sense of German nationhood long before German political statehood was formally achieved, and it is this element that helps condition West German thinking and actions. By the same token, it could be of concern to Moscow and East Berlin.

U.S. relations with East Germany have lagged behind U.S. ties with virtually other state of Central and Eastern Europe, although there has been some modest improvement in relations over the last several years. These have been hampered, however, by the shadow of the Wall and by long-standing problems like East German refusal to make good on compensation for U.S. properties in East Berlin and on Jewish claims strongly supported by the U.S. Congress. These have blocked not only better relations but also greater trade, which the GDR has sought. Nonetheless, periodic consultations between East Germany and the United States take place and the mood surrounding the relationship is considerably less negative than in the 1960s.

As a step toward better relations, Hermann Axen of the East German politburo visited Washington on an unofficial visit in May 1988. He was the most senior GDR official to come to the United States. He spoke in a conciliatory manner during his private meetings with U.S. officials. As a further signal for improved relations with the United States, the GDR in July 1988, after a meeting between Honecker and Jewish community leaders, announced that it had agreed in principle to compensate Jewish claimants.

The United States has been prepared to share or at least accept Bonn's positive assessment of the inner-German dialogue. It has particularly welcomed the end of Berlin crises and tensions as well as the improvement in travel and other exchanges between the two Germanies. It is more skeptical in its assessment of human rights progress in the GDR, but this is not as important an issue in U.S. domestic politics as human rights in Poland or Hungary. There should be no Bonn-Washington friction over this element of *Ostpolitik* unless the GDR insists on linking further progress in inter-German relations to East-West negotiations or unless it tries to use the talks to interfere with Western rights in Berlin or elsewhere.

Washington also has to remain highly sensitive to issues that might affect the status of Berlin. When Honecker in June 1989 received the newly elected Governing Mayor of Berlin, Walter Momper, and used the occasion to announce measures to make it easier for West Berliners to visit East Berlin,[46] U.S. officials could join West Germans and West Berliners in welcoming the improvement. But they also had to be concerned about the potential political implications of a separate negotiation between the authorities in West Berlin and the GDR. Honecker could, and perhaps would, use such talks to claim that West Berlin had a separate status from the Federal Republic and that the West Berlin government should function as a separate international authority, separate from West Germany and also from the authority of the allies. This could undercut the security of West Berlin by undermining its status as well as the justification for an allied role and presence, but it would be difficult for Bonn or even for Washington to object strongly if Honecker offered humanitarian improvements in exchange for political concessions.

Inter-German relations could, therefore, also complicate relations between the United States and the Federal Republic. They can have positive elements for both countries but they can also raise questions that could jeopardize security and status arrangements. There could, moreover, be serious frictions if the desire for closer inter-German links were to drive the Federal Republic into weakening its links to NATO defense. The United States now sees those links, and that defense, as elements of stability in Europe. Washington would not wish to see them changed except as part of a broader agreement that would provide at least an equal measure of stability for West Germany and Berlin, so that Americans could feel that they had not held their post-war trusteeship obligations in vain.

The steady development of inter-German relations was shaken, however, in the fall of 1989, when tens of thousands of East German refugees poured out via Hungary and West German embassies in Warsaw and Prague. The refugees were emotionally welcomed in West Germany, where there was also deep appreciation for the readiness of East European countries to let refugees pass through.

Although the GDR assented to the departure of the refugees for West Germany after some negotiations, the flight again demonstrated the fragility of the GDR and the powerful attraction of the Federal Republic. At the same time, it created problems for both East and West. Moscow again had to reflect about how to move toward an East

German regime and system that might reduce the inhabitants' tendency to flee. Washington had to recognize that West German public opinion will be ever less disposed to install nuclear weapons that can threaten Poland, Hungary, or Czechoslovakia, when those countries have helped East Germans to be free.

By stressing the impermanence of present arrangements, the flight also pointed to the need for other long-term solutions. Those solutions are still far from clear, and they will not be prescribed by Washington and Bonn alone, but they obviously could not be postponed forever.

The Dilemmas of Coordination

Bonn and Washington both expect at least several years of improving relations with the Soviet Union and Eastern Europe. After a short intermission at the beginning of the Bush administration, as the new President was undertaking a strategic review, both capitals have pursued broadly similar policies of accommodation with Moscow. The Federal Republic's policy receives more attention because of traditional concerns regarding German *Ostpolitik,* but Washington has made its own efforts.

The U.S. Chairman of the Joint Chiefs of Staff, Admiral William Crowe, visited the Soviet Union in the spring of 1989, as had the West German military Inspector General, Admiral Dieter Wellershoff.[47] The United Sates and the Soviet Union also signed an agreement to reduce the likelihood of war by accident.[48] U.S. trade restrictions toward the Soviet Union began to relax at the same time, in part because of greater Jewish emigration and in part because of the Soviet withdrawal from Afghanistan. America's subsidized grain sales rose to record levels. Even the restrictions on technology exports to the Soviet Union and Eastern Europe were becoming more relaxed, and there was talk of Moscow's receiving most favored nation trade treatment.[49] Several major U.S. corporations investigated joint ventures in the Soviet Union.[50]

When President Bush visited West Germany, he spoke at Mainz in very positive terms about the prospects for better relations with Moscow as part of the process of ending Europe's division. A visit by Bush to Moscow is under active discussion. He and other U.S. officials have suggested, in terms similar to those of German officials, that the West had an interest in Gorbachev's success. Bush also visited Poland and Hungary in July 1989 and offered not only U.S. aid but his personal support for a coordinated effort by the major Western nations.

Nonetheless, even as German-American policies toward the Soviet Union and Eastern Europe may be moving in parallel directions, there has to date been little coordination for several reasons:

- Germany and the United States have a different perspective. When Germans look toward the East, they see a traditional political, economic, and diplomatic relationship as well as a military threat. Many Germans believe that negotiations with Moscow on politics and economics can ease the military threat and can return Europe to a more stable and more balanced existence after the tensions of the world wars and the cold war. They believe that *Ostpolitik* can contribute to security. The Federal Republic is prepared to negotiate with Moscow about all these relationships and all these issues, and it hopes for a fundamental change in Europe. Washington is prepared to negotiate a global detente with Moscow. But the experience of the 1970s left many American political figures skeptical about prospects for real relaxation of tensions. Washington is always more ready than Bonn to exercise the principle of "linkage." Washington also does not see as clear a link as Bonn between security and *Ostpolitik*.
- Washington and Bonn have different wishes. The Federal Republic is prepared to have relaxation follow agreement; the United States wishes to have relaxation precede agreement.
- Washington and Bonn have different agendas. Bonn negotiates with Moscow on political topics or on topics that have a political consequence, such as CSCE or other broad European security arrangements. Washington negotiates on strategic arms or other weapons systems, in part because it is Washington that is responsible for NATO strategic security. This is another aspect of German-American complementarity. Both Bonn and Washington also want to negotiate with Moscow on trade, but Washington has traditionally been more concerned than Bonn about the danger that Western trade and credits could be used to benefit the Soviet military structure rather than the Russian people.
- There is also a different timing cycle. In Bonn as in Washington, governments like to go into elections with an East-West agreement to display as a sign of diplomatic effectiveness and of peace and stability. But German and American elections are now on opposite cycles, with the next German national election in 1990 and the next American Presidential election in 1992. Both want to have positive achievements during their elections years, and both want to make certain that the treaties reached during those years are on topics of particular interest to their citizenry. As many East-West negotiations require both German and American participation, each government must press the other to move toward accords in the area of greatest political benefit to itself and on a timetable that recognizes its political needs. Washington may well be con-

cerned about Bonn's readiness to make concessions on conventional and SNF forces in 1989 or 1990, as Bonn may be concerned about Washington's readiness to make concessions in 1991 or 1992.

Beyond these factors, there remain fundamental philosophical differences. In German *Ostpolitik,* there is an old and a new theme. The old is a recollection of German and pan-European history. The new is a contribution toward European stability and to the easing of Germany's division. Many Germans believe that there are strong pressures to return Europe to a situation analogous to that which existed before World War I, and that this will provide a broad framework for peace. They want to develop not only their own links to the East but also the entire European Community's, ultimately ending the division of Europe and generating a new structure of European contact, community, and security. Bonn also believes that Moscow will permit greater German links in Eastern Europe as well as expanded inter-German contacts only if Bonn is also talking to the Kremlin. Many Germans hope that overcoming the split of Europe will overcome the split of Germany.

But there are limits to *Ostpolitik.* If West Germany goes too far toward Moscow, to the point where the United States and other NATO allies believe that Bonn has turned to neutralism, it could lose its security arrangements and its leverage. Then, Moscow would have no further incentive to help ease inner-German human rights. West German officials recognize this. They try to chart a path that improves relations with Moscow without jeopardizing ties to the United States and other Western states, and without giving too much away too quickly.

The Federal Republic also has to reconcile divergent domestic opinions about *Ostpolitik.* Many Germans are ready to improve relations with Poland but are reluctant to make concessions that could prejudice a final German and Central European territorial settlement. Many also hold back when they see the enormous credits required to revive the East European and Soviet economies.

The biggest obstacle, however, remains Moscow's policy toward Germany itself. Gorbachev has dropped hints—but only hints—that the Soviet Union may be less firmly against German unity and against destruction of the Wall than in the past. That accounts in large measure for his appeal in Germany. But he has not taken concrete actions, and he has set no timetable for change. One German observer commented that Gorbachev had followed Soviet policy on Germany with more imagination and flexibility than in the past, but with equal toughness.[51] It remains to be seen, therefore, what Gorbachev can and will do in an area of immense importance to all Germans, and what price he may try to extract. If that price includes a reduction in the American security role, it raises many extremely difficult questions.

In American policy toward Moscow there is a different theme and a different drive. There is little sense of history because there is virtually no history except of tension and confrontation. Instead, the negotiations are conducted in the spirit of today and perhaps tomorrow, intensely practical, often focused on the minutiae of implementation and verification. They must pass not only the test of a U.S. executive review but must be weighed by a Congress that is never more skeptical than when it is presented with an East-West treaty. The Americans make a point of measuring Gorbachev's statements against U.S. perceptions of reality. Americans do not always understand the particular geographic and political pressures under which the Germans or other Europeans must negotiate with Moscow.[52] They tend to look more at Soviet military capacities than at military intentions, even if Reagan was prepared to state that Gorbachev's Russia was no longer the "evil empire."

Out of these differences must come a coordinated policy. Kohl has said several times that West Germany cannot be a "neutral wanderer between two worlds," and he reiterated that theme again strongly after Gorbachev's Bonn visit.[53] An alliance cannot function if some members are responsible for trade and accommodation while others are responsible for defense.[54] Moreover, West Germany cannot negotiate its own security protection with Moscow since history amply demonstrates that no state can give a credible guarantee against itself. By the same token, however, the United States cannot talk for Germany on Central Europe.

Washington and Bonn are now negotiating jointly and separately with Moscow and with East European states about the future shape of Europe and of the world, about the roles which they will play and which Moscow and East European states will play. But, even if they agree on one or another tactical aspect of one or another negotiation, they have no common concept about their goals and they have not even defined a joint framework. Until they do, the risk of German-American disagreements and misunderstandings remains an element in both countries' policies toward the East.

Notes

1. Henry A. Kissinger, *White House Years* (Boston: Little Brown, 1979), pp. 821–825.

2. Kissinger, *White House Years,* pp. 821–825.

3. *Financial Times,* October 25, 1988.

4. Text of speech in *Bulletin,* November 1, 1988, pp. 1268–1271.

5. Text of speech in *Bulletin,* November 1, 1988, pp. 1265–1268.

6. Text of statement in *Bulletin,* November 1, 1988, pp. 1271–1274.

7. *Financial Times,* October 26, 1988; List of agreements in *Bulletin,* November 1, 1988, pp. 1274–1276.

8. *The Economist,* October 29, 1988, pp. 50–51.

9. *Washington Post,* January 18, 1989.

10. Aspects of Gorbachev's visit are reported in *Frankfurter Allgemeine,* June 13 to 17, 1989, as well as in *FBIS, Western Europe,* June 12 to 19, 1989, and in *FBIS, Soviet Union,* June 13 to 21, 1989.

11. Text of declaration in *FBIS, Western Europe,* June 13, 1989, pp. 9–11, and in "Statements and Speeches," June 14, 1989.

12. List printed in *Handelsblatt,* June 15, 1989.

13. *Wall Street Journal,* October 21, 1988.

14. *The Economist,* April 22, 1989, p. 72.

15. *Financial Times,* June 20, 1989.

16. *The Economist,* June 17, 1989, p. 54.

17. "Deutschland-Nachrichten," June 21, 1989.

18. *The Economist,* October 22, 1988, pp. 53–54.

19. *Aktuelle Beitraege zur Wirtschafts- und Finanzpolitik,* October 18, 1988, p. 1.

20. *The Economist,* October 22, 1988, pp. 53–54; speech by Otto Graf Lambsdorff, Washington, February 6, 1989.

21. *Washington Post,* March 18, 1989.

22. The meeting was in Moscow, March 27 and 28, 1987, and recorded in *Die Beziehungen zwischen der Sowjetunion und der Bundesrepublik Deutschland* (Hamburg: Bergedorfer Gespraechskreis, 1987), hereinafter cited as *Die Beziehungen.*

23. *Die Beziehungen,* pp. 13, 20, and 32.

24. *Die Beziehungen,* pp. 38–39.

25. *Die Beziehungen,* p. 49.

26. *Die Beziehungen,* p. 32.

27. The meeting was in Bonn, December 3 and 4, 1988, and recorded in *Das gemeinsame Europaeische Haus—aus der Sicht der Sowjetunion und der Bundesrepublik Deutschland* (Hamburg: Bergedorfer Gespraechskreis, 1988); *Financial Times,* December 6, 1988.

28. U.S. worries are summarized in "Germany's Sly Fox," *Newsweek,* December 12, 1988, pp. 36–38.

29. Text of Genscher's speech in "Statements and Speeches," February 6, 1987.

30. Texts of Genscher's speeches in "Statements and Speeches," June 13 and October 4, 1988. The phrase that Genscher used in German was "Gorbachev beim Wort nehmen," which has been translated to mean either "to take Gorbachev at his word" or "to hold Gorbachev to his word," with the first translation being used for the first speech (even in the West German official translation) and the second for the later speeches.

31. As in Genscher's speech to the Davos World Economic Forum on January 29, 1989.

32. Lambsdorff speech of February 6, 1989, in the U.S. Senate Caucus Room, p. 10. Lambsdorff made similar statements in meetings with U.S. officials on the same visit.

33. *Washington Post,* June 22, 1989; *Washington Times,* June 22, 1989.

34. "The Week in Germany," June 23, 1989.

35. *Documents on Germany, 1944-1985* (Washington: U.S. Department of State, 1986), pp. 1059–1064.

36. *Documents on Germany,* p. 1088.

37. *Innerdeutsche Beziehungen: Die Entwicklung der Beziehungen zwischen der Bundesrepublik Deutschland und der Deutschen Demokratischen Republik 1980-1986* (Bonn: Bundesministerium fuer Innerdeutsche Beziehungen, 1986), pp. 26–37. The statistics on inter-German travel can be confusing because they are often interpreted to mean the number of visitors from East to West. In reality, they give the number of visits, and that number might be larger than the number of visitors because one person might travel several times. Moreover, many of the statistics, especially on permits issued, are based on East German, not West German, sources; the GDR records the number of permits it issues but the West German authorities can not record every visit.

38. *Frankfurter Allgemeine,* April 11, 1987.

39. "The Week in Germany," December 2, 1988, p. 1; "Deutschland-Nachrichten," December 7, 1988, p. 7; *Wall Street Journal,* January 31, 1989.

40. *FBIS, Eastern Europe,* March 31, 1989.

41. *Financial Times,* March 1, 1989.

42. West German reports on contacts with the GDR are in Dorothee Wilms, *Deutschlandpolitische Bilanz 1988* (Bonn: Bundesministerium fuer innerdeutsche Beziehungen, 1989), and in speech by Ottfried Hennig on "Konzeption und Zwischenbilanz der Deutschlandpolitik," *Bulletin,* May 4, 1989, pp. 375–380.

43. *FBIS, Eastern Europe,* March 15, 1989, p. 15.

44. *Frankfurter Allgemeine,* March 13, 1989.

45. Summary of main points of Honecker visit is in *Jahresbericht 1987* (Bonn: Bundesministerium fuer innerdeutsche Beziehungen, 1988).

46. *Frankfurter Allgemeine,* June 20 and 22, 1989.

47. *Washington Post,* June 22, 1989.

48. *Washington Post,* June 8, 1989.

49. *Financial Times,* June 14, 1989; *Washington Post,* March 13, 1989.

50. *Wall Street Journal,* March 30, 1989.

51. Guenther Gillessen, "Der Herr im Europaeischen Haus," *Frankfurter Allgemeine,* July 3, 1989.

52. Fritz Stern, *Dreams and Delusions* (New York: Knopf, 1987), p. 224.

53. *FBIS, Western Europe,* June 16, 1989, p. 9.

54. *Bulletin,* November 23, 1989, p. 3.

7

Contrasting Economic Philosophies

The Crash

The shattering crash on Wall Street in October 1987 not only reflected grave concern about the American economy. It also signalled widespread apprehension about the fragility of the global financial system, about the contradictions and dislocations that had developed within that system, and about the inability of the leading economic powers to coordinate and concert their actions.

Although the list of causes for the market implosion could go on at length, it was clear that one catalyst was the growing divergence between American and German economic policies. The picture of an American Secretary of the Treasury publicly denouncing one of America's principal allies while that same ally proceeded apparently undisturbed to the implementation of policies directly at variance with Washington's wishes helped bring on the crisis of confidence that provoked the crash.

The setting for the crisis had focused special attention on German and American policies. The U.S. current account deficit had not declined a great deal in 1987 despite some improvements in the balance of trade. The U.S. Federal Reserve system ratcheted U.S. interest rates rapidly during 1987 to protect the dollar, continue attracting foreign capital, and fight inflation. As it did so, the German *Bundesbank* raised its own rates. That policy was intended to protect Germany from inflation and to stop further capital flows to the United States, but it raised American fears that its own rate increases would be constantly nullified by German actions. The spiral of rate hikes that might ensue could jeopardize prosperity everywhere and perhaps cause a financial crisis throughout the industrialized world.

The American Secretary of the Treasury, James Baker, singled out the German actions for special criticism, even though other countries were also raising their rates, because it appeared that the German action triggered others.[1] The United States thought German fears of inflation were greatly exaggerated. The Germans, in return, accused the

United States of using Germany as a whipping boy. They also questioned the accuracy of the American analysis of events.[2] The President of the German *Bundesbank,* Karl Otto Poehl, later pointed out that the German rate increase was merely intended to keep pace with U.S. rate increases, but German determination to keep that pace helped to unsettle the markets.[3]

The divergence between German and American economic policies, and the crash that it helped provoke, underscored one of the most baffling dilemmas of the present international system: how can Western governments maintain an open global economic system while pursuing separate and sometimes divergent macroeconomic policies at home, and how can they continue to cooperate if most of their economic decisions—even those with profound international repercussions—are made mainly on the basis of domestic rather than international considerations?

The crash also showed the particular tensions generated when two of the principal economies of the world, the American and the German, function on the basis of very different economic traditions, philosophies, and policies, and when either has the power not only to oppose but even to render ineffective the policies of the other.

German Ghosts and Realities

Despite the supposed rationality of economic theory and analysis, economics remains a science haunted by ghosts, ghosts of policies past and, particularly, of failures past. Germany and America are haunted by different ghosts, floating into consciousness from opposite directions. They also have different, and even opposite, economic traditions and attitudes.

The ghost that haunts Germany is the memory of the great inflation of 1923 which ravaged and embittered the German middle class. The German mark, worth eight to the dollar in 1919, had collapsed to an exchange rate of 4,200,000,000,000 to the dollar at the peak of the inflation. One of the legacies of that inflation was that the charter of the *Bundesbank,* when the bank was established after World War II, specifically instructed the bank to preserve the value of West Germany's currency.

Beyond the ghosts, German economic and financial attitudes and policies have their roots in the totality of German history. Subjected to centuries of political, military, and economic turmoil, Germans have sought security and preservation of assets more than risk-taking for future profit.[4] Divided in medieval times into small and often poor states, they placed great stress on the development of crafts and of labor-intensive production as well as on the quality of their products. Government, industry, and agriculture cooperated closely to encourage exports, which were absolutely essential to minuscule principalities depending on trade to supply the many necessities not available within their narrow borders. This laid the foundations of today's German neomercantilism and of its concept of close collaboration between government and business.

The German Empire under the Hohenzollerns continued the traditions of autarky and government-business collaboration. It established a wide-ranging social welfare system to gain trade union tolerance for its costly military build-up and for production processes that worked severe hardships on the workers. The emerging giants of German industry demanded long apprentice periods for promotion and stressed pride in quality of workmanship. The mercantilist drive found expression in German ambitions for global economic influence as an instrument of national power and prestige. The German Empire took great pride in the symbols of its new industrial might.

Out of the ruins of the German Empire and later of Hitler's Third Reich grew yet another set of psychological imperatives. Many Germans lost everything either in the hyper-inflation of 1923, the great depression that followed, the wars, the bombings, the foreign invasions, or in the suppressed inflation after World War II when American cigarettes and Parker pens became the most sought-after instruments of exchange. These disasters set the stage for the sweeping currency reform of 1948 when the Reichsmark was abolished and Germans were given forty Deutschmarks (DM) each to start a new life and to build a new prosperity for themselves and their country. They also set the stage for the Marshall Plan and the free market "economic miracle" that were to follow.

As the Federal Republic grew, the traditions of government-industry collaboration again came into their own. The last pieces of the present structure were put into place by the Social Democratic coalitions of the 1960s and 1970s with an extensive—and expensive—system of social welfare and government-subsidized health and job security arrangements that is described as "the social net" because it catches and protects whoever happens to fall.

Going back to the medieval tradition of government concern for the unfortunate and of a strong role in the economy, various systems of German government involvement and supervision have established a complex web of rules, regulations, and subsidies that often discourage enterprise, innovation, and initiative.[5] The Federal Republic has also preserved the conviction that German economic performance would be one of the most important standards by which the country would be measured in the world.[6]

Out of this experience emerges the powerful and dynamic but deeply conservative German economy of today. It values steady prosperity without inflation, moderation—if necessary at the expense of growth—and smoothing of the economic cycle by avoiding excess. It seeks incremental productivity gains and production growth through investment and the promotion of exports. It stresses individual worker responsibility for a product. Contrary to the United States, it selects its managers from technical and engineering rather than financial backgrounds, producing a class uniquely dedicated to highest quality production.

This set of philosophical constructs has given Germany a reputation as a reliable manufacturing state, inflation rates well below the global average, relatively restrained domestic demand, exports as a significant percentage of gross national product, and some protection from the extreme effects of cyclical economic swings. It resembles Japanese more than American economic philosophy and management, although it is not as centralized as "Japan, Inc." It has made West Germany the world's largest exporter, ahead of either the United States or Japan, and a powerful element in international finance and investment. Some German exports, especially machine tools, have such a high reputation for quality that the demand for them has become virtually inelastic.

Many Americans still recall the "economic miracle" of postwar reconstruction when they think of West German economic performance since World War II. But German growth over the last two decades has lagged. Despite its efforts to smooth the economic cycle, Germany has suffered some effects from two global recessions over the past 15 years, especially because of its dependence on foreign markets and foreign supplies (mainly petroleum and natural gas).

During much of the 1980s, German domestic demand lagged behind many other industrialized countries.[7] So did output and employment. By 1987, unemployment had risen to the nine per cent level. Workers rarely relocated to find new employment because the social net tooks care of their needs. Industry, like labor, was also slow to react to shifts in the economic environment. By 1988 and 1989, however, German growth rates again surged, to levels of 3.5 per cent a year, principally because of strong domestic and international demand for capital goods.

The West German economy also suffers from structural imbalances. A number of inefficient nineteenth century industries, such as steel, shipbuilding, and coal, remain directly or indirectly subsidized. Although some, like steel, have recovered substantially from their low points, they are still not the robust core elements of the economy that they once were. Many modern high-technology plants have established themselves in the South, but heavy bureaucratic regulations make it difficult and costly to start a business or to attempt any new economic activity. Almost all areas of the country support inefficient agricultural production for political reasons and insist that the federal government protect them from food imports—which it usually does through the European Community mechanism.

Thus, Germany's most efficient industries are geared and motivated to compete abroad, while the least efficient are somewhat sheltered from foreign competition. There can be no better formula for export growth, and that export growth has compensated for restrained domestic demand. It has done so especially in recent years because the global capital boom has expanded German machine tool production and exports.

Despite these problems, German productivity, efficiency, and stability have created immense affluence and influence. Visitors to Germany comment admiringly on the widespread prosperity that the country and its people enjoy.[8] Like any export-based prosperity, however, it depends on the consistent ability of the nation and of its capital and labor force to maintain their competitive spirit and edge. It also depends on the willingness and the ability of others, including the United States, to continue to purchase German products.

The West German currency is a powerful element in the global economy. More than 17 per cent of the world's currency reserves are held in DM, second only to the 64 per cent held in the dollar and continuing to rise.[9] The German economy dominates the European Community, and Germany has a sharply rising export and current account surplus with other Community countries. The European Monetary System is in many respects a DM zone, with countries deliberately joining it to come under the influence of the stable and consistent policies of the *Bundesbank,* although they may pay a price in terms of slower immediate growth.

American Ghosts and Realities

It would be difficult to find two peoples with greater differences in traditional economic attitudes than the Germans and the Americans.

The United States was established by persons and groups fleeing regulation and seeking unfettered opportunities. Economic venture was one of the essential expressions of personal freedom for many of them. Most immigrants abandoned the guild and craft tradition. Few restrictions existed in the new land. Great natural resources, open markets, and almost unlimited labor, all beckoned. Those who tried a new idea could often succeed. If they failed, it was not a crime to have tried, or to try again, in a new and even perhaps in the old setting. In contrast to Germany, there was little or no government guidance, and usually no government support, although the links that farmers and businessmen had with their Washington representatives led periodically to the imposition of tariff barriers. This combination has given the U.S. economy great vitality, flexibility, and capacity for growth and innovation, but it also spawns risks and uneven development as well as violent cycles.

The American market and American resources were so immense that for most of U.S. history few elements of the industrial economy regarded exports as necessary or even useful. There was no obligation to pursue autarky, as the country was economically self-sufficient without special effort. Many laws governing economic activity were written as if the United States economy represented a closed system, not subject to the rigors of the international market-place or global competition. American watchwords were growth, opportunity, and concentration on abundant domestic markets and resources. The efficiencies of mass production and mass domestic sales cast American economics into modes of thought almost opposite to German. Germans sought prosperity in exports; Americans sought it in the domestic market. German policy would restrain domestic demand; American policy would exalt it.

Whereas Prussia, the German Empire, and even the Federal Republic consciously pursued economic power as an element of national influence, the United States rarely if ever thought in those terms. To most Americans, global economic power was a by-product of their prosperity, not sought as an end in itself but accepted as it came. Only in rare instances, as in petroleum extraction, international airline affairs, or defense production, have major sectors of the U.S. economy consistently sought and obtained government support for international operations. By the same token, few Americans have in the past seen any reason to pursue policies that might jeopardize domestic growth in order to preserve international influence.

America also has its ghosts. Not the inflations that the Germans experienced, but the depressions, particularly the great depression that lasted from 1929 into the 1930s. Those depressions, resulting from over-expansion of credit and the subsequent collapse of the banking system, have been and remain constantly on the minds of American economists and political leaders as well as of almost every American citizen. The United States has tried to prevent depressions, and even recessions, mainly through monetary and fiscal policies intended to manipulate domestic demand. It has welcomed, enjoyed, and even sought, the dynamic upward forces of the economic cycle, while also trying constantly to find ways of avoiding the downward forces generated by that same cycle.

The United States is the world's single largest economy. It has dominated the international economic system since World War II. In the years immediately after World War II, it was so powerful that it was virtually a law unto itself. Then, many economists feared that the "dollar gap" based on an overwhelming American export surplus would never be relieved.

More recently, however, as other economies have grown in Europe and Asia, the American economy has become vulnerable. It has already proceeded through considerable restructuring as its traditional heavy industries have lost market share to the newly industrialized countries. It has, however, compensated by developing new areas of production and by expanding its service sector. The United States still represents the world's largest market for many foreign as well as domestic producers, maintaining relatively open borders to foreign manufactures and foreign investment although the pressures for sector protectionism have grown significantly in the last several years and the 1988 Trade Act has generated some objections from the General Agreement on Tariffs and Trade.[10]

The American economy has since World War II been more subject to economic cycles than the German, with both growth rates and interest rates fluctuating more rapidly than German rates. Despite a severe recession from 1980 through 1982, it has grown more rapidly than the German economy during most of the 1980s and has created a total of almost eighteen million new jobs during the decade.[11] It has done this despite the many upheavals it has undergone. It has helped sustain demand by tax cuts and deficit financing on an unprecedented scale that has created genuine concern not only in the United States but in international banking and financial circles. At least part of the deficit has been covered by foreign—including German—investment either in U.S. production facilities, equities, or government and industrial obligations.

From the standpoint of international coordination, it often matters little whether German or American policy is objectively "right." No matter who may be right, the contrast between their policies can annul their effectiveness and can even jeopardize the stability of the global financial system as well as the two countries themselves.

The Global Economy

Elements of the Western financial environment are now more interdependent than ever. Currencies and capital flow quickly and freely from country to country, to the degree to which the Western world has become virtually a single system for financial transactions. Decisions made in any single financial center have an immediate impact not only on one country but on many.

That global system suffers, however, from a number of problems that could generate serious trade and financial imbalances: excess productive capacity in many traditional industrial products; wide-ranging exchange fluctuations; high indebtedness, among both developed and developing states; and uneven national growth and inflation rates. The system requires constant monitoring and cooperative management if it is to be kept stable and prosperous.

Despite their differences, the United States and the Federal Republic have tried to work together during the two distinct periods of international finance since World War II. During the Bretton Woods era of officially fixed exchange rates against the U.S. dollar, they collaborated in the coordinating mechanism of the International Monetary Fund (IMF). To avoid exchange rate crises generated when the DM was stronger than its official exchange rate, the Federal Republic and the *Bundesbank* worked closely with the United States to attempt to preserve the value of the dollar. The *Bundesbank* intervened periodically to help defend the dollar. Unlike France, which shifted its currency reserves increasingly from dollars into gold, the Germans kept most of their reserves in dollars. The Federal Republic also agreed to make "offset" payments, purchasing U.S. Treasury obligations and U.S. military equipment to compensate the United States for the exchange losses that it suffered by maintaining large forces in Germany.

After the Bretton Woods system collapsed, the current system of floating rates began, with exchange rates decided by market forces. American and West German officials have actively participated in the meetings of finance ministers and central bankers of the principal financial powers. The United States and the Federal Republic were in the initial group of five, known as the G-5, along with France, Great Britain, and Japan, and later in the G-7 after Canada and Italy were added.

Although the floating system is nominally intended to function through the interplay of market forces, Bonn and Washington along with other leading economic powers have consistently attempted to guide the extent and the direction in which currencies should fluctuate. They have done this not only through the G-5 and G-7 but also through periodic senior-level meetings usually named after the places at which they convened. The first of these meetings, held in 1973 at the Smithsonian, set a broad framework for the floating system. The two most prominent recent meetings, at the Plaza (September 1985) and the Louvre (February 1987), were intended respectively to push down the value of the dollar and to establish trading ranges for the principal currencies.

The Federal Republic helped found another coordinating mechanism, that of periodic summits between the heads of government of the world's principal financial and trading powers. These summits were initiated by Chancellor Helmut Schmidt of Germany and President Valery Giscard d'Estaing of France to provide a forum for leaders to exchange ideas on global economic issues privately in an informal setting, to coordinate their policies, and to set broad directions. They have, however, become large and rather unwieldy exercises. They often do not so much develop a consensus as attempt to mitigate the effects of policy differences. They have also often gone well beyond financial and economic topics, and therefore no longer serve the purposes for which Schmidt and the West German government had originally initiated them. They do not lead to permanent solutions, especially because governments often go their own different ways between meetings.

Complementarity

In economic as in strategic matters, Washington and Bonn have developed a genuine complementarity, although the economic one is unplanned. The United States has become an important market for many of the world's goods, including products from Germany and its European Community partners. Indirectly or directly, it stimulates global demand. It has done this, however, at least in part through the fiscal deficit that sustains and even expands demand but that also generates a disturbing long-term debt burden.

The Federal Republic profits from that market, either by its own exports or by those it sends to other states that may in turn export to the United States. A special study has shown that U.S. economic policies during the 1980s, including the trade deficit, have boosted prosperity in the entire industrialized world.[12] Germany has in turn helped sustain the American market by being prepared to finance a portion of the American debt. But the size of the U.S. credit burden risks generating long-term tensions and unacceptable mutual dependencies over time even if most German investment and credit in the United States now comes from private rather than government funds. It puts the American economy at risk because of its high dependence on foreign—including German—credit. It puts the German economy at risk because it exaggerates even further Germany's high level of dependence on foreign markets. It has also helped draw funds from Germany as part of a pattern of outward capital flows that in 1988 hit record proportions.[13]

Current Coordination

The economist Henry Wallich once defined coordination in international economic affairs as "a significant modification of national policies in recognition of international economic interdependence."[14] It would, therefore, reflect a determination to put the interests of international economic coordination ahead of purely national economic goals and philosophies. Theoretically and ideally, of course, such a dichotomy should not even exist, although it does. National governments and central banks should be able to select policies that would not only be in the interest of their own country but would also support common global economic objectives.

To encourage policy coordination, the Organization for Economic Cooperation and Development (OECD) has for some time made recommendations to both the United States and Germany. It has recommended that the United States reduce its fiscal and foreign exchange deficits, and has specifically indicated that this would require "additional budgetary action." It has recommended that the Federal Republic make microeconomic and structural reforms to help promote greater non-export growth.[15] Such measures should include a reduction in government regulations and in subsidies, as well as tax reform. The OECD has also warned that adjustment should not be left exclusively to the exchange markets.

Within or outside the G-7 meetings and summits, U.S. and German officials have said the same things to each other as has the OECD. The Germans have consistently recommended that the United States reduce its budget deficit to restrain demand, cut imports, and ease the upward pressure on interest rates. The United States has urged an increase in the German growth rate and structural reforms that would ease German dependence on exports and would promote German imports of foreign—including American—products.

The German economy in 1988 did succeed in making at least some of the policy adjustments that had been proposed by the OECD and by the United States. The annual growth rate, which had averaged only 1.7 per cent from 1980 through 1987, accelerated to 3.4 per cent.[16] The number of unemployed fell below 2 million for the first time in seven years. But unfortunately, at least from the standpoint of global trade balances, exports contributed somewhat more to growth than did domestic consumption, with a jump in exports to other European Community states.[17] The trade surplus for 1988 was DM 128 billion, a significant increase over 1987, and the current account surplus was DM 85 billion, also higher than 1987.[18] The export contribution to growth as calculated by the German Economics Ministry was 60 per cent, somewhat lower than in other years but still substantial.[19]

Although the *Bundesbank* attributed the higher jump in the growth rate to a rise in domestic as well as in export demand, it also noted that the gradual decline in the German current account surplus had been arrested after the end of 1987.[20] It warned that further depreciation of the D-Mark had to be resisted because the earlier decline had contributed to the export rise.[21] But another expert study warned that even after 1989 further growth in the German economy would come more from exports than from domestic consumption, with exports to rise more than imports,[22] and various studies indicated that the German trade and current account surplus would rise even further for 1989.[23]

The rise in German domestic consumption that had been sought by the United States had not materialized enough to help ease the imbalances between the two economies, despite tax reforms that had lowered direct German tax rates. The statistics indicated that other countries in Europe had pulled the German economy upward more than the other way around, although indirect and spill-over effects would be very difficult to measure accurately in a system as intricately linked as that of the European Community.

Whatever the causes for the German growth rate increase, it began to worry the German monetary authorities around the end of 1988— especially because of a jump in inflation around the turn of the year. There were periodic rumors that the *Bundesbank* would increase interest rates. It finally did so during the spring of 1989, although not as early as some had expected and with some uncertainty about the impact it would have immediately on the growth rate.[24]

The United States, like the Federal Republic, has made some progress in removing some of the disparities in the relationship between the two economies and in fulfilling some of the recommendations of the OECD, but not all the problems have been solved and several do not yet appear to be near solution.

The U.S. growth rate has slowed and continues to slow, and the U.S. trade deficit declined in 1988. American exports of capital goods have surged, having risen by over 50 per cent in two years.[25] Nonetheless, the decline in the dollar had not boosted exports as much as many had hoped, and the dollar had begun to rise again by the latter half of 1988 and through 1989. The trade and current account deficits remained troublesome. There was also deepening concern about a resurgence of inflation.[26]

The most serious problem, for psychological as well as economic reasons, was that the U.S. Federal budget deficit remained at a very high level. For Fiscal Year 1988 it stood at $155 billion, higher than in Fiscal Year 1987. Although the totality of the government debt, whether state, local, or Federal, may have declined as a share of U.S. Gross Domestic Product,[27] it remained a severe drain, especially given the low U.S. savings rate. Large portions of the Federal and state budgets had to be dedicated to interest service on the national debt. It also presented a constant risk to exchange rate stability because it had to be financed at least in part by foreign investors.

The Fiscal Year 1990 budget, which Bush presented to the Congress in February 1989, projected a deficit around $100 billion, but many economists questioned its projections for growth and inflation. They feared that errors in those projections could lead to a much greater deficit and much greater dependence on foreign investment, leading in turn to a weaker dollar.[28] As the economy developed during 1989, those fears deepened. Although tax revenues remained somewhat higher than expected, the tendency for additional budget expenditures continued unabated.

Different parts of the U.S. government continued to pursue different economic objectives and often contradictory policies. The administration, anxious to promote growth, favored low interest rates and no increase in taxes to solve the fiscal deficit. The Congress, reluctant to cut programs—especially on the domestic side of the budget—wanted a tax increase in order to cut the fiscal deficit but did not wish to initiate one. The Federal Reserve, wishing to curtail inflation and recognizing that this could be done only through monetary policy, needed to have higher interest rates.

The U.S. policy dilemma is almost paralyzing because there are many conflicting objectives and very little room for maneuver.

With respect to the U.S. dollar, the United States wishes to avoid having too strong a dollar in order to prevent U.S. exports from pricing themselves out of the international market. But it needs a strong dollar to restrain inflation and to encourage foreign investors to help finance the budget deficit.

With respect to that budget deficit and interest rates, the United States needs low interest rates to keep the economy going, to sustain tax revenues, and to reduce its debt service expenditures and help reduce the deficit. But the United States cannot afford to permit its boom to go into an inflationary cycle, so it must raise interest rates to slow the economy. On the other hand, if interest rates were to rise too high, the dollar would become too strong, exports would fall, debt service would cost too much, and tax revenues could fall sharply if a recession were to follow. Finding the right course for the U.S. economy is now brutally difficult, and the margins for error are slim.

Genuine philosophical differences have helped to complicate the search for a common American policy. The "Keynesian consensus" of the 1960s has shattered, leaving in its place a mixture of post-Keynesians, monetarists, supply-siders, pragmatists, and others. There have also been differences about economic policy in the Federal Republic, reflected in a long 1987–1989 dispute about tax policy and in some uncertainty about interest rate boosts in early 1989,[29] but none of those disagreements are as fundamental as those that have prevailed in the United States.

The matter of timing may become crucial. A number of problems that could perhaps be resolved in five to seven years by gradual methods, and which might perhaps be best addressed by such gradual methods, may not get the benefit of that much time. Instead, they may need to be solved more quickly to maintain international and mutual German-American confidence, but a fast solution may be more risky than a slow one.

Even more cruelly, as the 1987 crash demonstrated, mistakes could be costly for all concerned. The imbalances in the global financial system have become serious enough that a mistake by any of the partners—especially by such major partners as the United States or the Federal Republic—could trigger serious problems and perhaps a collapse of the system.

German bankers and businessmen worry privately that the American financial system and the dollar could collapse, but they must also try to do what they can to stop it from happening because such a collapse could also have a very severe effect on Germany. And the steps they might wish to take to protect themselves could bring about precisely the outcome they fear.

Trade and the European Community

Even in an economically interdependent world, one vital area of economic activity is not open: trade. Unlike capital, goods do not move freely. Many countries practice overt or subtle forms of protectionism or trade promotion. Hidden and indirect import controls often supplement or replace more traditional tariff barriers. These disruptions of free trade have helped to cause and may have even aggravated the problems posed by global financial movements because they impede some of the traditional corrective mechanisms from functioning. Moreover, recent trends have moved away from, rather than toward, freer global trade.

Trade relations between the Federal Republic and the United States have also come to represent an increasingly troubled area with the potential for conflicts of interest. Those relations are not purely bilateral, because Germany is a member of the European Community, but they have a strong bilateral element because Germany is such a powerful force within the Community and its policies carry weight.

Three problems in particular have become acutely sensitive:

- Trade in agricultural products, an area in which the United States has a considerable cost advantage but in which the Community countries have erected a series of barriers to protect their politically powerful farmers. Washington and Bonn have both tried to avoid making a crisis of this issue, but there is strong public sentiment on both sides, especially in the farming communities and their representatives.[30]
- Within the general argument about agricultural trade, there was a potentially serious conflict about a Community ban on beef with hormone supplements, such as U.S. beef. That ban, which took effect at the beginning of 1989, was regarded by the Community as a health measure and by the United States as a protectionist device. The United States retaliated against Community products when the ban was put into effect.[31] The problem demonstrated the dichotomy between German political interests in good relations with the United States on the one hand and German interests in domestic agricultural production on the other. German farmers and environmentalists played an important role in promoting the European Community ban on American beef, but German officials tried to prevent the dispute from turning into a major crisis once the United States had retaliated.[32] After the U.S. retaliatory measures took effect, both sides were able to find at least a temporary compromise, but the suddenness and the intensity of the dispute reflected the growing sensitivities on both sides and especially on the American.
- The United States has long complained that the subsidized European production of Airbus represents unfair competition against U.S. airframe manufacturers. This is very much a German-American issue as well because a center of Airbus production is in Bavaria and the late Franz-Josef Strauss was an avid proponent of separate European aircraft production. A 1988 German decision to authorize a further multi-billion DM subsidy for Airbus provoked a sharp attack from Clayton Yeutter, then U.S. Trade Representative.[33] The Germans said that the Airbus subsidy represented no unfair competition because the United States subsidized its aircraft manufacturers through military research and production contracts. They also argued that the United States should not

complain about the Airbus because significant portions of Airbus production were in the United States and because Boeing could not even keep up with its own production orders. Nonetheless, the Airbus remained an open issue that continued to fuel U.S. resentment.

The United States has also become alarmed over the possibility that European Community plans for an internal market by 1992 could represent a "Fortress Europe" that would exclude American products from the continent.[34] German officials insist that this is not their intention and that they are working hard to keep the Community open to global trade.[35] This has not in itself fully eased U.S. concerns, but those concerns have not risen to the crisis stage and need not do so if, as 1992 approaches, firm signs of an open European Community continue to appear.

The entire trade discussion is carried out against the background of increasing sentiment for trade retaliation within the U.S. Congress, which in the summer of 1988 passed a new Trade Act intended to give the U.S. government in general and the U.S. Trade Representative in particular the authority and even the direction to act with considerable force on behalf of U.S. exports—if necessary by retaliatory measures. A specific warning was addressed to Europeans, but the Europeans rejected the American charge.[36]

The German role and weight within the Community could come to constitute a particular problem in the German-American dialogue. The Community represents the Federal Republic's principal trading outlet. There is a major and growing German surplus within the Community, consistently tens of billions of DM per year.[37] As more than half of West German exports go to the Community, many West Germans feel comfortable in the Community and sense less urgency to resolve their differences with the United States and others. Germans may believe that the Community offers a secure environment that can purchase the German production surplus even if trade with other parts of the world stagnates.

For the United States, however, the Community all too often appears as a privileged arrangement that individual European states use to protect their inefficient domestic producers without accepting national responsibility for their actions. This American sentiment has helped embitter the disputes between Washington and the Community, as in the matter of the beef hormones, and has spilled over into Washington's relations with Bonn.

Prospects for Future Coordination

The global financial system and the many meetings held at many levels have not been able to solve the fundamental problem created by the impact of divergent national policies on the international environment. Such mechanisms as exchange rates and interest rates can compensate, but they cannot carry the full burden of adjustment indefinitely. Sooner or later, states and central banks come under ever greater pressure to review their policies.

This becomes all the more important as the partners become more equal. From being based on U.S. dominance, the international financial structure must increasingly be based on greater collaboration between near equals. Yet the United States still wants to pursue policies congenial to its own traditions and perceived needs. And the Federal Republic has to date given little indication that it is prepared to adjust its own policies. There are many reasons to question whether the transition from an American-dominated global financial structure to a more balanced one can be completed without generating financial instability. A badly managed transition can be risky for all partners, whether they are gaining or falling in relative influence.

There are, therefore, real dangers if present trends continue. If the Federal Republic persists in its export drive without a compensating readiness to buy foreign goods and without expanding its domestic market more vigorously, it could undermine the very currency and market on which global—as well as German—prosperity still depend. If the Americans persist in budget and trade deficits, U.S. assets and U.S. Treasury debt financing might only be attractive to foreigners at escalating interest rates. If both countries do not coordinate their policies to a greater degree, they could stimulate capital and speculative flows that could undermine the stability of the entire global financial structure.

The OECD recommendations suggest that both countries could undertake certain steps that would not only benefit their domestic economies but would also help stabilize the international financial system. To date, however, neither the Federal Republic nor the United States has been prepared to take those steps although each is somewhat less reluctant than it used to be.

On the German side, the philosophical origins of German policies appear difficult and perhaps impossible to overcome. In the United States, equally profound difficulties exist. Recent U.S. elections suggest that a U.S. President can only be elected by promising not to raise taxes, but that a Member of the U.S. Congress can only be elected by promising to provide more programs for constituents. Such pressures can produce deficit financing almost indefinitely. Moreover, they have political rather than economic origins and may not be subject to economic argument unless and until the economic situation deteriorates severely.

It is by no means certain that true international coordination can come about only if countries pursue policies that sacrifice domestic objectives for the sake of a stable international system. It may be possible to find policies that serve both domestic and international purposes even for countries with different attitudes and traditions. To date, Washington and Bonn have not been able to find policies consistently intended to serve both objectives. Although they have still succeeded in cooperating most of the time, it remains to be seen if this can continue as their roles and weights shift further.

Trigemony

There has been some discussion about possible Japanese-American "bigemony" in managing global financial policies and their coordination. But such a system cannot succeed because it ignores the Europeans and the European Community as well as the Germans, who are the principal economic and financial power in the Community. Therefore, the smallest form on which any global system can effectively be based must be a trigemony, with the three partners being the United States, Japan, and the Federal Republic.

The true test of their coordination may yet lie ahead, when the current prosperity slows and when national governments and central banks are under even greater pressure to protect themselves and their immediate interests than they have been during the boom times. After the 1987 crash, the *Bundesbank,* the Federal Reserve, and the Japanese acted quickly and jointly to prevent the crash from turning into a world-wide financial collapse. This was an essential and important step, but did not guarantee that they would be able to coordinate in a similar manner if a problem was more prolonged.

The German government and the *Bundesbank,* like Japan, have shown that they can participate and grow prosperous in a system dominated by the United States, in which the Germans have a growing but still not primary role and in which they have often balanced U.S. policies. It remains to be seen whether German policy can be equally effective as their own role becomes more powerful. The conservative policies and the disinflationary bias of German economic management may work less well as Germany becomes a primary determinant of global policy. Neo-mercantilism and reliance on foreign markets may not be feasible once a state becomes a dominant partner, since there is a risk of exporting deflation precisely to those countries where one wishes to market. By the same token, it is not at all certain that the United States could manage its own policies and guide its own prosperity effectively in a system in which it is no longer at the center.

The German-American dialogue about macroeconomic policy is now troubled by all these considerations as well as by the obligation to work ever more closely together. The two governments and central banks are not fully free to do all the things that the other wishes and perhaps even needs, and neither is fully free to do as it might wish for itself.

All three governments are under tight domestic and international constraints in a situation that is potentially unstable. Yet they are also intricately bound to each other, and they cannot escape from their mutual obligation to coordinate and to adjust. And for the Germans and the Americans, whose relations go much wider than the economic realm, the dilemma remains particularly baffling.

Notes

1. *Frankfurter Allgemeine,* October 17, 1987.

2. *Frankfurter Allgemeine,* October 19, 1987.

3. Karl Otto Poehl, "Cooperation—A Keystone for the Stability of the International Monetary System," Arthur Burns Memorial Lecture delivered at the American Council on Germany and the Atlantik-Bruecke, e.V., New York, November 15, 1987, pp. 9–11.

4. Norbert Walter, *West Germany's Economy* (Washington: American Institute for Contemporary German Studies, 1987), pp. 4–16; "Accepted Economic Paradigms guide German Policies," *IMF Survey,* November 28, 1988, pp. 1–4.

5. Arthur F. Burns, *The United States and Germany* (New York: Council on Foreign Relations, 1986), pp. 19–32.

6. Otto Wolff von Amerongen and Hans-Dietrich Genscher, "Stabile Wirtschaft: Grundlage aussenpolitischer Gestaltungskraft," Hans-Dietrich Genscher, ed., *Nach Vorn Gedacht . . .* (Bonn: Bonn Aktuell, 1987), pp. 113–122.

7. Organization for Economic Cooperation and Development (OECD), *OECD Economic Surveys: Germany, 1987/1988* (Brussels: OECD, 1988), p. 19.

8. John Ardagh, *Germany and the Germans* (London: Hamish Hamilton, 1987), pp. 145–161.

9. Deutsche Bundesbank, *Report for the Year 1988,* pp. 62–63.

10. *Financial Times,* February 14, 1989.

11. U.S. Council of Economic Advisers, "Economic Report to the President," January, 1989, p. 346.

12. The study was conducted by Jeffrey Shafer for the OECD, and reported in the *Washington Times,* September 18, 1988.

13. *Wall Street Journal,* February 14, 1989.

14. Henry Wallich, as quoted in Jacob A. Frenkel, Morris Goldstein, and Paul R. Masson, "International Coordination of Economic Policies: Scope, Methods, and Effects," Wilfrid Guth, moderator, *Economic Policy Coordination* (Washington: International Monetary Fund and Institut fuer Wirtschaftsforschung, 1988), p. 149.

15. OECD, *OECD Economic Outlook 43* (Paris: OECD, 1988), pp. vii–viii. The recommendations were forcefully reiterated a year later, in *OECD Economic Outlook 45* (Paris: OECD, 1989), pp. vii–xvi.

16. *Wall Street Journal,* January 12, 1989.

17. *Financial Times,* September 28, 1988.

18. *Wall Street Journal,* February 14, 1989.

19. "Aktuelle Beitraege zur Wirtschafts- und Finanzpolitik," November 21, 1988, p. 7.

20. *Monthly Report of the Deutsche Bundesbank,* September, 1988, pp. 36–37.

21. *Ibid.*

22. A study for the West German D.I.W. predicted export growth at 9 per cent and import growth at 6 per cent for 1989; see *Handelsblatt,* June 29, 1989, and *Frankfurter Allgemeine,* June 22, 1989.

23. *OECD Economic Outlook 45,* p. 74; *Report of the Deutsche Bundesbank for the Year 1988,* p. 27.

24. *Financial Times,* June 30, 1989.

25. *Wall Street Journal,* November 23, 1988.

26. *OECD Economic Outlook 45,* pp. 59–64.

27. *Wall Street Journal,* November 16, 1988.

28. *New York Times,* February 10, 1989.

29. *Financial Times,* May 23, 1989.

30. For background, see Carlisle Ford Runge, "The Assault on Agricultural Protectionism," *Foreign Affairs,* Fall, 1988, pp. 133–150; and *New York Times,* October 19, 1988.

31. *New York Times,* November 30, 1988.

32. *Financial Times,* December 29, 1988; *Wall Street Journal,* January 20, 1989.

33. *Frankfurter Allgemeine,* November 4, 1988.

34. For a summary of plans for the internal market, see European Community, *Europe without Frontiers—completing the Internal Market* (Brussels: European Community, 1988).

35. Remarks by Ludolf von Wartenberg, Parliamentary State Secretary in the German Economics Ministry, Washington, March 28, 1988.

36. *New York Times,* November 2 and 20, 1988; *International Herald Tribune,* November 14, 1988.

37. *Report of the German Bundesbank,* July, 1987, p. 14.

8

New German and American Attitudes

A Visitor to Berlin

Early on the morning of June 26, 1963, a long motorcade began the drive from Tegel airport in the French sector of Berlin toward the center of the city. The first official limousine, right behind the police escort motorcycles and cars, carried President John Kennedy and Governing Mayor Willy Brandt. Dozens of cars and buses followed, bearing the White House staff, Washington officials who had accompanied Kennedy, Berlin or West German officials who received and escorted them, and other American and German personnel who had some connection with the visit.

Many Berliners stood along the sidewalks to greet the American President and to shout a welcome as the motorcade advanced. This seemed like nothing particularly striking for a Presidential visit, although the crowds were larger than usual. Members of the U.S. party, self-styled hard-bitten political operators, took it in stride. Some joked that it would be nice to be able to bring back the Berliners to vote in the United States. Others observed that the same people now cheering them might only twenty years earlier have cheered Hitler. Crowds and adulation were routine to the Kennedy White House, and were calculatedly taken in stride. This visit seemed no different from many others.

As the column wound its way through the city streets, however, it became clear that this was not the usual political crowd, drummed together by party retainers or grudgingly given a few hours to provide a colorful backdrop for yet another parade or festival. One by one, the Kennedy staff and other Americans fell silent in awe. Even the leaders of the convoy, Kennedy and Brandt, looked at each other in deepening amazement as they responded to the ceaseless shouts and applause. The crowd grew larger and larger, almost blocking passage except for narrow lanes through which the motorcycles and cars could squeeze.

Every single Berliner who could walk, and some who could not, had come to greet the American President and, through him, to thank the nation that had stood by them during the postwar crises, the blockade, the Wall, and Khrushchev's threats. The East Berliners on the other side of the Wall watched on Western television, listened on the radio, or else tried to come as close to the Wall as the police would allow to hear the reaction of those who saw the motorcade.

When Kennedy spoke from the balcony of the Schoeneberg city hall, masses of people jammed the square in front of him and stretched as far as the eye could see along the streets converging from every direction. They greeted Kennedy with an immense roar. They interrupted his speech time after time with deafening cheers and applause, especially when he said that the citizens of Berlin, like the citizens of ancient Rome, should be filled with pride that they could say "Ich bin ein Berliner."

Nobody who was there will ever forget that day. No chief of state or government, no public figure, could dare to hope for such a welcome. Kennedy himself told the White House staff afterwards that "We will never have another day like this as long as we live."[1] But the Berliners were cheering a foreigner, an occupier, the leader of a state that had defeated them and had assented to the division of their country and even of their city.

The Kennedy visit marked the apogee of German popular response to the presence of Americans in Germany and to the alliance between the two countries. Six months later, Kennedy lay dead. So, three weeks before him, lay Ngo Dinh Diem, the President of the Republic of Vietnam whose assassination forced the United States to turn its attention from Europe to Asia and from deterrence to war. But the visit, and the Berliners' response to the President and to the United States, symbolized German gratitude for the conqueror who had stayed to help and to protect them.

The Berlin crises in themselves had not alone created that enthusiasm. It had its origins in the early days after the war, when American soldiers began helping the Germans whom they had been instructed not to befriend, when the American public sent millions of Care packages to feed the German people through the harsh postwar winters and through the many days of hunger, need, and humiliation as the country lay in defeat and in ruins. When the mass of the German people began to learn, through the Nuremberg trials and other revelations, of the ghastly crimes that had been committed in the name of Germany and even by their countrymen, the American readiness to forgive and to help those who had not been guilty came as a redeeming gesture in a world of destruction and disgrace.

When the Americans helped protect Berlin and Germany against Stalin's Red Army through the Airlift and the U.S. guarantee, and when they also gave candy to the children, it was for many Germans as if a long nightmare had ended and a new spirit had entered the scene to help them rise to their feet and to give them another chance.

The Americans reciprocated. The Berlin blockade, more than any other single event, transformed the image of the Germans, and especially of the Berliners, from enemy to friend. It was in large measure the plight of the Berliners, and their courage in the face of the blockade, that provided in the United States the popular support for the return of U.S. forces to Europe and ultimately for the NATO commitment.

Americans also appreciated what they saw as the triumph of their own values. They saw West Germany grow strong because it had become a democracy, and it had learned democracy from America. The Germans had adopted the American system and had proven not only themselves but the system. When the communists, whether Stalinist or Maoist, proclaimed themselves the wave of the future, West Germany was a beacon of reassurance. In the Germans the Americans saw images of themselves, of their own hardship and triumph, of trial and redemption. The many Americans of German origin felt a special pride. And Kennedy's "Ich bin ein Berliner" had such an electrifying effect because it responded to the tacit identification of so many Germans and especially Berliners with the United States.[2]

Out of the experience of the postwar years grew an emotional as well as a political bond between Germans and Americans. It was a bond that was not only forged through the common experiences of the postwar years, through American generosity, German gratitude, and American appreciation in turn. It also combined a strong element of the national interest of both countries. The Federal Republic needed a protector. Many political figures in the Federal Republic, including Adenauer, wanted a strong Western connection that would help foster the Western elements in German culture, philosophy, and politics. The United States in turn saw that it would need a solid and stable base in Western Europe to help meet the threat from the Soviet Union.[3] But the emotions aroused by the postwar association provided a powerful underpinning for decisions that might be made for reasons of state, and on occasion even dictated those decisions.

New German Attitudes

Forty-five years after the end of the war, German feelings are different. Many attitudes have changed. And they have changed in ways that must be regarded as potentially worrisome for the German-American relationship and that have even been termed "estrangement."[4]

German attitudes have become more mixed, less easy to catalogue or to evaluate. Some of the attitudes seem contradictory. They warrant careful examination, especially because of those apparent contradictions.

Surveys conducted in 1986 and 1987 showed that West German public opinion strongly favored NATO, and by a margin of ten to one wished the Federal Republic to remain a member of the alliance.[5] Support for NATO was confirmed by a 1988 poll which showed a ratio of 76 to 13 between those who believed NATO was needed as against those who believed it was not.[6] That ratio, curiously, was exactly the same as it had been in 1969, and more positive than in 1973, 1982, or 1987, though weaker than during much of the 1970s or in 1983 and 1984.

Surveys have also consistently shown that well over three quarters of West Germany's population wish to keep American troops "to improve the protection of freedom." They have also shown that three out of four West Germans oppose total or partial withdrawal of U.S. forces.[7]

Nonetheless, surveys have also reflected genuine German dislike for some NATO practices, such as low-level flights over West German territory, and for the presence of nuclear weapons on German soil. They have shown widespread opposition to modernization of NATO short-range weapons and, in one survey, have put national defense lowest on a list of seventeen national priorities. One survey put the Soviet Union on an equal basis with the United States, crediting Reagan and Gorbachev with being equally serious in their wish for peace.[8]

A 1988 public opinion survey in the Federal Republic presented an even more negative picture.[9] That survey showed that most respondents (51 to 28 per cent) had a more positive judgment toward current Soviet policies than toward American policies, and fewer (13 to 28 per cent) had a negative judgment of Soviet then American policies. The policies in question mainly dealt with national security, the most important area of German-American collaboration.[10]

The survey reported that 84 per cent of the respondents had positive reactions toward Gorbachev, whereas only 53 per cent had positive reactions toward Reagan.[11] The survey also reported that only 24 per cent of the respondents regarded the Federal Republic as threatened by the Soviet Union, as against 55 per cent who thought it was not threatened.[12]

In several instances where these and other surveys attempted to make distinctions based on the age and education levels of the respondents, they showed that younger and better educated Germans were somewhat more likely to be critical in their attitudes toward the United States and favorable toward the Soviet Union. For example, the percentage of those having greater confidence in the Soviet Union than in the United States in response to a 1987 survey was higher among those under thirty years of age, although not dramatically.[13]

Experts have long believed that the arrival of the "successor generation" in West Germany would lead to a less friendly German attitude toward the United States. The Germans who had not experienced the postwar years would not share the feelings of gratitude toward the Americans.[14] Instead, their attitudes would be shaped by U.S. involvement in the Vietnam conflict, which was widely condemned in Western Europe, by Watergate, by the "malaise" of the late 1970s, and by what the West Europeans perceived as U.S. unilateralism in the 1980s. That conclusion is borne out at least to some degree among the surveys.

Other surveys, however, concluded that the major factor that appeared to be creating changes in West German attitudes was not the emergence of a "successor generation." Instead, those surveys suggested that attitudes toward national security issues, and with them attitudes toward the United Sates and the Soviet Union, corresponded more to the respondents' political affiliations than to their age.[15]

Whatever the reasons, many surveys showed that even America's friends in West Germany had some questions about U.S. policies, about American lifestyles, and about U.S. capacity to lead the West at the present time. The attitude was not confined to the extremes at the German Right and Left or to groups that might be expected to be anti-American. Persons who have long been supporters of the United States, and still are, worry about U.S. policies and performance. One survey, for example, indicated that only 6 per cent of all West Germans regarded a "Made in America" label as a sign of good quality.[16] The United States is clearly not the model that it was in the postwar years.

Travels around West Germany reinforce the impression given by the surveys. In one after another conversation, anywhere in the Federal Republic, Germans express their concern about whether the United States is prepared to do what is necessary to maintain its preeminent place in the rapidly shifting global strategic, political, and economic environment. They also worry that the United States may be turning to the Pacific and that U.S. friends in Europe, such as the Federal Republic, may be abandoned. They think that they have to begin to look for other connections before the United States decides to leave.

More than anything else, Germans complain that U.S. policies are in constant motion and are not only unpredictable but almost capricious. They complain that this makes it impossible for America's friends to know what to do. They also sense that the United States all too often takes Germans for granted and expects them to do whatever one or another Washington bureaucracy wishes. Even if one discounts some of these conversations as manifestations of a classical German tendency toward pessimism, they reflect a sober and widespread German feeling that the United States is not the reliable partner that it was, and that the United States does not always follow policies that suit German interests. These attitudes reduce German readiness to take advice, to listen, and to do what Washington wishes. That new sense of independence, more perhaps than any other single element of German opinion, is most pronounced among the young.

These opinion trends have coalesced into a kind of wariness about U.S. policies and about America itself. A German scholar, Arnulf Baring, cited surveys showing that many Germans thought that there was really no difference between the two superpowers and that the United States was also an "aggressor."[17] Some Germans, he wrote, have also concluded that the Atlantic alliance makes the Federal Republic nothing more than a U.S. "satellite." Such attitudes are not only shared by intellectuals and the Greens, but also by elements of the Social Democratic Party and by nationalists such as the *Republikaner.*[18] Baring, citing this as a new German "megalomania," said that anti-Americanism had become a "proper code of behavior" among some groups and that it was accepted as normal and as a sign of political identity.

Some of these tendencies are not new. There have almost always been German-American divergences of opinion on certain aspects of their collaboration, such as strategy, and especially on the use of nuclear weapons. Some of these issues presented particular difficulties for German public and political opinion for a long time. The "Yankee go home" and *"ohne mich"* campaigns of the 1950s, or the *Kampf dem Atomtod* demonstrations of the late 1950s, were as violent as any antinuclear campaign of the 1980s, especially because they reflected the intense wave of anti-military sentiment that swept across West Germany after the defeat in World War II.[19]

Because of the intensity of such campaigns, and their efficient and dedicated organization, it has always been difficult to judge the depth and breadth of the popular attitudes supporting them. All too often heavily committed groups have created impressions of German opinion that proved to be unrepresentative. The massive campaigns against the Pershing II and Ground-Launched Cruise Missiles in the early 1980s fizzled once NATO governments initiated actual deployment of the systems. But they nonetheless also reflected genuine popular reservations about certain policies.

Public opinion in any one country should not be analyzed in a vacuum. Many of the positive attitudes about Gorbachev, or the negative attitudes about Reagan, are matched in the United Kingdom and France and are distinctly not only German phenomena.[20] In numerous evaluations about attitudes toward Washington and Moscow, British and French opinion inclines as much or more toward the Soviet Union than German opinion, or is no more strongly supportive of NATO.[21] For example, more West Germans than other West Europeans believe that a U.S. presence in Europe is necessary to deter attack.[22] A recent Emnid Institute poll in North-Rhine Westphalia found that the United States was second only to France among countries that the respondents found "likable to very likable."[23]

As important as the evidence of pure numbers, of course, is the strength of conviction with which any particular attitude is held. This is difficult to analyze in statistical terms, but certain impressions do emerge. One such impression is that German public opinion now concentrates much more intensely on the prospects for the European Community than on further NATO collaboration. West Germans welcome the evidence that Europe is taking shape, first in the form of a West European entity but also later in a pan-European sense, and they clearly appreciate that this will have a significant impact on their lives. They sound much more animated when they speak of these phenomena than when they speak of NATO or of the trans-Atlantic association, even when they believe that the latter are important.

Many Germans find prospects for closer ties with Eastern Europe and the Soviet Union highly stimulating. They talk about openings for travel, trade and contacts. They are clearly pleased that the threat from Moscow may perhaps have turned into an opportunity, even if they do not yet perceive clearly what that opportunity might represent.

The polls and conversations present a mixed picture. There is little "anti-Americanism" in the narrow sense. In fact, many Germans—especially among the young—remain fascinated by the United States as a phenomenon and as a culture. German public attachment to the NATO alliance and to the American connection remains very strong. Most West Germans do not want to be cast adrift on some neutralist path. Nonetheless, the view of the United States has become more skeptical, more critical, and certainly more distant. West Germans believe that the United States no longer has the answers to their problems and may in many areas not have the same objectives as the Federal Republic, but they still want to maintain the alliance with America.

The greatest German doubts and reservations were about individual U.S. policies. The policies that were questioned, such as military maneuvers or nuclear weapons deployment, were often tied to military security but also to East-West matters. The polls in which the United States fared worst reflected disagreements about particular policies; the polls in which the United States fared best reflected the broad German desire for a continued tie with America.

If the emotion expressed for Kennedy and the United States has gone, it has been replaced by a more self-assured sense of German interests, by questioning and by a readiness to search for different policies, not by a wish to separate from the United States.

New American Attitudes

Americans, like Germans, have changed their thinking on many issues. Those changes have not gone as deep as those in West Germany, largely because the changes in America's situation between 1945 and now have not gone as far as those in Germany. Nor are U.S. attitudes on Germany as closely documented as West German attitudes toward the United States and toward U.S. policies. But there are changes in American public opinion attitudes and those must have an impact on Bonn-Washington ties.

Like most Germans, most Americans have remained remarkably constant in their attitudes on the fundamentals of international affairs over the past several decades.

In particular, most Americans continue to believe that the United States must play an important world role. The periodic surveys conducted by the Chicago Council on Foreign Relations show that 64 per cent of those polled want the United States to continue to play an active part in the world, as against 27 per cent who want to stay out.[24] Another survey, conducted by several other organizations, confirmed the finding by showing that only four per cent of the respondents wanted to retreat to a policy of defending only North America.[25]

With respect to specific goals, the American public seemed generally to take positions that agreed with the attitudes and even the interests of the Federal Republic. Decisive majorities favored arms control, containing communism, and defending the security of the allies.[26]

Attitudes toward the Federal Republic, and toward U.S. defense commitments, also remained highly supportive. The Federal Republic was third on a list of countries toward which Americans had positive feelings, behind only Canada and Great Britain but ahead of other NATO states.[27] It was listed fourth among those countries in which the United States was considered to have a vital interest, after Great Britain, Canada, and Japan, and rated even higher in leader opinion.[28] Moreover, four fifths of all respondents indicated that they wished to keep U.S. forces in Europe, three fifths were in favor of maintaining the U.S. commitment to NATO, and almost two thirds favored sending U.S. troops in response to a Soviet invasion of Europe.[29] The survey reflected no popular foundation for the often heralded shift in American public opinion to Asia, or for neo-isolationism.

Nonetheless, as a warning of potential German-American, or European-American, disputes, the survey showed that over three quarters of all respondents regarded "protecting the jobs of American workers" as the single most important foreign policy goal of the United States.

There were also signs that Americans were beginning to worry more about the costs of defense at a time when some allies were not making what the Americans regarded as a parallel contributions. A very strong majority of 86 per cent of respondents feared that Americans could do their economy serious damage by spending too much to defend other countries.[30] With respect to foreign competition, almost 60 per cent of the respondents to one survey agreed that "economic competitors pose a greater threat to national security than military adversaries do, because they threaten our jobs and economic security."[31]

Other surveys reported frustration about the policies of U.S. allies. Even though the surveys showed that most respondents favored continuing ties to Western Europe and stationing U.S. forces there, they also reported strong majorities who believed that allied defense contributions were too small and, in particular, that U.S. allies had not done enough in the struggle against international terrorism and in the operations against Libya.[32]

Worries about America's economic situation surfaced during the 1988 Democratic Party presidential primary campaign of U.S. Representative Richard Gephardt, who argued that more should be done to protect U.S. producers and to curtail foreign investment in the United States. That campaign was defeated, but Democratic Presidential candidate Michael Dukakis echoed some of Gephardt's themes in the closing weeks of his own campaign. Elements of those campaign themes persist and the worries remain alive, especially in areas and industries hard hit by foreign competition at home or feeling unfairly restricted in their capacity to compete abroad.[33]

There is also a "successor generation" in the United States, and it is also growing. Those are persons who did not experience German-American cooperation in the postwar years, the Berlin blockade, the early German-American links, or all the common experiences that marked the establishment of NATO and of the Western security structure. They saw Vietnam and they now see European-American differences on many issues such as trade and East-West relations. Many do not travel abroad or, when they do, go more to England or France in Europe or to Asia. Like Germans their age, they cannot be expected to assimilate all that has happened in German-American collaboration. Unlike Germans, however, they can expect to reach positions of influence and power quickly because of the nature of the American political process. They have not aroused the interest of German-American scholars as much as the German "successor generation" has, but they will be a factor in future relations and in U.S. policies.

What emerges is a picture of a nation that remains fully committed to its international obligations and specifically to the Atlantic relationship. Nonetheless, given U.S. economic difficulties and the shift in American public threat perceptions, the surveys indicate that the United States will increasingly be inclined to turn its attention inward and to concentrate more on its economic requirements. American public opinion need not turn isolationist. But the United States could be less prepared than before to expend itself for foreign obligations when it appears that there may be more important problems to solve at home. It would remain to be seen how much of the desire to yield burdens would be accompanied by a readiness to yield direction.

American opinion has thus evolved in directions that parallel the evolution in West Germany. Like most West Germans, most Americans remain fully supportive of the NATO alliance and of the basic German-American relationship. Both publics know who their friends are. But, as in the Federal Republic, American attitudes on some specific policy issues are moving in directions that can create alliance frictions and German-American divergences. On the German side, the greatest potential divergences would result from German fears of nuclear weapons on West German soil; on the U.S. side, they would result from American concerns about unfair economic competition and unequal alliance burdens, from a belief that U.S. allies are showing no appreciation for U.S. protection.

Some of the differences in mutual attitudes result from the evolution of the German-American agenda. During the immediate postwar years, German and American public and political opinion concentrated on the cold war crisis in Central Europe and found in each other not only necessary but also good partners. Now the agenda is more global, less concentrated on military threats but on diplomatic coordination, East-West accords, economics and trade. The Federal Republic and the United States may need each other just as much in these areas as in the earlier ones, but their interests do not fuse as clearly and the need for cooperation is not so obvious even to an informed public.

Even when the publics in both countries experience similar phenomena, such as "Gorbomania" or an easing of the Soviet threat, Germans and Americans may come to different conclusions but with a similar effect. West German public opinion feels that NATO preparedness is less vital. American public opinion sees less need to contribute to allied defense. The shifting moods in each country find their way into the political dialogue of the other, reinforcing hesitation on both sides.

American public attitudes toward West Germany, therefore, in some ways resemble West German attitudes toward the United States. They remain positive, but they also bear the seeds of future disagreements.

The German Wish for Reunification

There is an aspect to German public opinion that has no parallel in the United States. It can, however, have an impact on German-American relations. It is the urge in the Federal Republic for German unity.

The strength of that urge is difficult to evaluate. As a factor in German consciousness, even if not in daily speech, it may be reminiscent of the French attitude on the loss of Alsace-Lorraine after 1871: "Speak of it never; think of it always."[34] American and even German analysts have periodically consigned it to insignificance, asserting that West Germans were so interested in their prosperity or in their West European attachment that they had forgotten German unity. That has never been correct.

Reunification remains a theme in German thinking. One German scholar said that this German urge should be regarded as a natural impulse for the German people, and part of the consciousness of the German identity.[35] It remains an objective for the German nation. Chancellor Kohl's advisor Horst Teltschik observed in May 1989 that the German question was "more current than ever."[36] It remains on the minds of Germans on both sides of the Wall, even if they do not expect reunification to come about soon.

After the detente negotiations, reunification became a less immediate objective in the 1970s. Public opinion surveys indicated that those who perceived it as an urgent goal of West German policy fell from 45 per cent to about 2 to 3 per cent between 1966 and 1971-1972.[37] But other surveys have shown that reunification remains a long-term objective for between 70 and 80 per cent of all West Germans, and one poll showed that a majority of 78 per cent regarded the Germans in West and East Germany as a single people.[38] As Teltschik had observed, it remains a genuine and current issue.

The desire for unification, or for overcoming some of the effects of division, must therefore be a factor in German policy. It is a principal purpose of Bonn's inter-German policy. And, to the extent to which West Germans link inter-German prospects with broad East-West relations, the desire for better contacts between all Germans and for improving human rights in the GDR becomes an element pressing

Bonn in relations with the Soviet Union and other states of Central and Eastern Europe. Many Germans believe that there can be no European unity without German unity, and that progress toward human rights in Eastern Europe will bring about progress toward human rights in the GDR. One of the reasons for Gorbachev's popularity in Germany is the widespread belief that he will make contacts between East and West Germany easier and that he will also permit—and perhaps encourage—more human rights in East Germany.

The question of German unification could also become an issue in German domestic politics, as any open political question can. It therefore cannot be neglected or forgotten in German-American relations, and the United States could damage its position in German public opinion if it appeared to be the power opposing progress toward German unity.

This appeared all the more true in the fall of 1989, when the flight of tens of thousands of East German refugees through Hungary and through West German embassies in Eastern Europe again showed the ultimate logic of German unity. The flight also raised the "German question" in dramatic human form and showed that the ideal of a united Germany retained immense power over all Germans.

The Interaction of Attitudes and Policies

There can be little comfort in the strong evidence that Germans and Americans still want to maintain a close association despite divergent views about many policy matters. Policies have an impact on opinion, as well as vice versa. If too many policies differ, they can produce a change in attitudes. A reservoir of mutual sympathy is not a permanent or immutable asset, and it might not survive long or deep policy differences. A split in German-American opinion could follow, even if neither country might wish it, and the balance of positive opinion could become a balance of negative opinion. That would constitute a risk to the relationship because it could make it harder for the two countries to collaborate in the many areas where they still have common interests.

The most important question, therefore, is whether German and American political and public opinion would accept a greater degree of divergence on specific policies without turning to wider mutual irritation and hostility, and without forgetting the common interests that remain. This question does not appear in the public opinion surveys because it is too hypothetical to pose. But the answer to that question may decide the state of German and American opinion about each other over the 1990s and beyond, and it will help shape prospects for continued collaboration.

Notes

1. McGeorge Bundy, *Danger and Survival* (New York: Random House, 1988), p. 390.

2. Fritz Stern, *Dreams and Delusions* (New York: Knopf, 1987), p. 222.

3. George F. Kennan, "After the Cold War," *New York Times Magazine,* February 5, 1989, p. 33.

4. Harald Mueller and Thomas Risse-Kappen, "Origins of Estrangement," *International Security,* Summer, 1987, p. 52.

5. Inger-Lise Skarstein, rapporteur, "Interim Report of the Sub-Committee on Public Information on Defence and Security," North Atlantic Assembly, November, 1988, p. 44.

6. *Public Opinion,* May/June, 1989, p. 21.

7. *Public Opinion,* May/June, 1989, pp. 45–46.

8. *Public Opinion,* May/June, 1989, pp. 47–50. The information on the low rating for national defense priorities was reported in the *Washington Times,* December 15, 1988.

9. Gesellschaft fuer Sozialforschung und Marktforschung mbH, Sinus, *Soviet and American Policies in the Opinion of Germans in the Federal Republic of Germany,* a study commissioned by the Friedrich-Ebert Stiftung and Stern Magazine (Munich: Sinus, 1988).

10. Sinus, *Soviet and American Policies,* p. 12.

11. Sinus, *Soviet and American Policies,* p. 18.

12. Sinus, *Soviet and American Policies,* p. 11. The surveys of the North Atlantic Assembly over five years showed a consistent trend toward greater credibility for the Soviet Union after Gorbachev had come to power.

13. Stephen F. Szabo, "Public Opinion and the Alliance," Paper presented to the 1988 meeting of the International Political Science Association, Washington, August 20, 1988, Table 6.

14. Stern, *Dreams and Delusions,* p. 222.

15. Hans Rattinger, "Change versus Continuity in West German public Attitudes on national Security and nuclear Weapons in the early 1980s," *Public Opinion Quarterly,* Winter, 1987, pp. 495–521.

16. American Broadcasting Company, "Good Morning, America" broadcast, January 6, 1989.

17. Arnulf Baring, *Unser Neuer Groessenwahn* (Stuttgart: Deutschland Verlags-Anstalt, 1988), pp. 129–134.

18. Baring, *Unser Neuer Groessenwahn,* pp. 136–145

19. Josef Joffe, "Europe and America: The Politics of Resentment," *Foreign Affairs, the United States and the World, 1982,* p. 569.

20. *Public Opinion,* March/April, 1988, pp. 29–30, and May/June, 1989, pp. 21–29.

21. Ben J. Wattenberg, "Bad Marx: How the World sees the Soviets," *Public Opinion,* March/April, 1987, pp. 9–11.

22. Szabo, "Public Opinion and the Alliance," Table 8.

23. "The Week in Germany," November 25, 1988, p. 7.

24. John E. Rielly, ed., *American Public Opinion and U.S. Foreign Policy, 1987* (Chicago: Chicago Council on Foreign Relations, 1987), p. 11.

25. Daniel Yankelovich and Richard Smoke, "America's 'New Thinking'," *Foreign Affairs,* Fall, 1988, p. 6.

26. Yankelovich and Smoke, "America's 'New Thinking'," p. 12.

27. Rielly, *American Public Opinion,* p. 18.

28. Rielly, *American Public Opinion,* p. 17.

29. Rielly, *American Public Opinion,* pp. 21, 22, and 32.

30. Yankelovich and Smoke, "America's 'New Thinking'," p. 8.

31. Yankelovich and Smoke, "America's 'New Thinking'," p. 13.

32. *Public Opinion,* March/April, 1989, pp. 30–34.

33. *Washington Post,* December 5, 1988.

34. Stern, *Dreams and Delusions,* p. 229.

35. Werner Weidenfeld, "Ratloses Nationalgefuehl: Fragen an die Deutsche Frage," Weidenfeld, ed., *Nachdenken ueber Deutschland* (Koeln: Verlag Wissenschaft und Politik, 1986), pp. 11–15.

36. *Wirtschaftswoche,* May 25, 1989, p. 21.

37. Elisabeth Noelle-Neumann, "Im Wartesaal der Geschichte," Weidenfeld, ed., *Nachdenken ueber Deutschland,* p. 135.

38. Gerhard Herdegen, "Perspektiven und Begrenzungen," *Deutschland-Archiv,* December, 1987, pp. 1261–1263.

9

Present at the Dissolution?

The ice has become thinner than many think.

—Volker Ruehe

The Old and the New

When U.S. Secretaries of State James Byrnes, George Marshall, Dean Acheson, or John Foster Dulles traveled to Europe decades ago, the "German Problem" was on their minds. They had to think about it and talk about it at every stop. So it was in February, 1989, when the newly appointed Secretary of State James Baker made his first European tour.

But Baker was not worrying about how to protect West Germany from Moscow. He was worrying about how to keep West Germany from getting too close to Moscow. And he was not worrying about the Germans being too weak and dependent, but about their being too strong and independent.

The "German Problem" has changed for America, as well as for others. The Germans have advanced from being a pawn in the East-West chessboard to being a principal player in all the things that matter, be they military, economic, or diplomatic. Moreover, they and the Americans represent the only countries that can rightfully claim that they have a central role in each and every one of those three areas.

West Germans can be proud of that progress. As President von Weizsaecker observed, the Federal Republic may not be a great power but it must have a hearing.

Americans can also be proud. The United States has done more than any outside country to make the new Germany possible.

But success has brought its own problems. It threatens to obscure the basic interests that first brought Bonn and Washington together. It has brought to the fore many issues that the two countries must address but on which their views do not fully match.

As this study showed, there are very basic differences in certain American and German approaches, and they are not likely to disappear. The two countries have different economic philosophies. They have different geographic situations. They see Russia differently. They have different attitudes on nuclear weapons stationed in Europe. They each want to negotiate with Moscow, and they each worry when the other does.

The study also showed disputes that arose out of a failure to communicate or to understand, not out of an objective difference. The most recent, and most dramatic, was over sales of chemical manufacturing equipment to Libya, where Bonn did not pay enough attention to American thinking (and to its own announced policy). Another was over the U.S. concept of "discriminate deterrence," which failed to give adequate advance thought to the likely German and European reaction. Other examples abound, on both sides.

Persons on both sides also sometimes act out of frustration. When American officials decided to leak information about German sales to the Rabta plant, or when Chancellor Kohl decided to give a newspaper interview postponing a decision on modernizing missiles, they were going public because they felt that their previous private statements and signals had not been understood, or had perhaps not been taken seriously.

Count Lambsdorff observed during his visit to Washington in January 1989 that Germans and Americans talk much more about each other than to each other. That is certainly true. More important, even when they do talk to each other they often do not listen to what they hear.

But there are many instances in which the two countries have helped each other but received little credit. It was the Germans, more than any others, who told Moscow that the United States and Canada belonged in the "European home." It was an American President who personally shifted the U.S. position on SNF negotiations to take account of West German domestic and strategic needs.

Moreover, basic German and American public opinion toward each other is still highly positive, even if those same publics differ on the specifics of policy. And there is a genuine sense in both countries that they are members of the same community of values.

It is this dichotomy that both countries now face. Washington and Bonn agree that security now means more than military force, but they have not agreed on the proper balance of military, diplomatic, and economic components. They agree on the broad objectives of global economic coordination, but they have not agreed on the specifics of their own macroeconomic collaboration. They agree on better relations with Moscow but have not reconciled their approaches.

As a result, the two countries are diverging from each other in their policies and even in the perception of their interests. And this divergence is more profound than other disagreements in the past because the two countries have changed as has the world in which they live.

Some of that divergence is inevitable, for all the reasons cited in this study. It may even be essential and desirable, if the alternative is to keep the relationship as it was decades ago. It need not lead to a divorce.

Future Roles in Europe

Europe, in the future as in the past, is the most important area for future German-American collaboration, and also the area with the greatest potential for disagreement.

The West Germans see a revived and renewed Europe, East and West, and they see opportunities to establish Central European relations that can mitigate the effects of their division.

The Germans do not want the United States to leave the "common European home," but they have not fully calculated how to conduct an opening to the East without losing their backing in the West.

The United States also perceives a new situation in Europe, but is much less certain what it means. Washington has also not yet seen how the United States can or should fit into a new pan-European pattern.

Mikhail Gorbachev has opened both opportunities and traps for Europe and America. The opportunities include the re-creation of Europe in a form that is both stable and open. The traps include Western arguments about how to handle his offers and about how to shape that new Europe.

If Gorbachev did not exist, he would have had to be invented. He offers Washington and Bonn, as well as all of NATO, an opportunity to reduce their accumulation of weapons and manpower in Central Europe without diminishing their security. But he does not offer it only as a favor to them.

Gorbachev is now negotiating simultaneously, but separately and on different topics, with Bonn and Washington. But those two capitals and other NATO nations have not yet calculated how to factor these talks into their common needs. Nor have they agreed on how NATO defense and diplomacy can be made to work together, not against each other.

Politicians and statesmen everywhere are trying to find ways to assure the Soviet Union that they will not threaten its security interests in Eastern Europe. But nobody appears to recognize that the United States has legitimate security interests in Western Europe, and that those interests serve other states as well—including the Federal Republic.

The compact of the 1940s and 1950s was that Germany would give up unity, at least for a time, and the United States would give up isolation. It was the only way German and American statesmen saw to keep a part of Germany free and to keep the United States in Europe. To a degree that Americans have not understood, the Germans have never accepted division but have constantly worked to ease or end it.

Now Bonn sees opportunities for easing the division further. Those opportunities may or may not be real, but the relation between those opportunities and the old compact has not been consciously considered, except perhaps in Moscow.

The Western allies, and especially the United States and the Federal Republic, have not yet agreed or even decided separately about the roles that they want and expect to play in the new European order, and how they can continue in that new order a relationship that is different from today's but that remains friendly and mutually supportive.

In that new order, the German and the American roles must be different from those that they have played for forty years, and the collaboration need not be as intimate or as pervasive. But it is not desirable or even necessary that they should separate.

If Bonn and Washington can agree on the re-shaping of the European order, and if they can collaborate with their NATO and other partners, they can almost certainly cast it to their wishes. But nobody will do it for them.

Roles in the Global System

Beyond Europe, however, lie broader questions regarding the shaping of the global system and international society. Those questions become more and more important as the world becomes increasingly interdependent in economics, conservation, arms proliferation, and in other areas as well as in war and peace.

The United States shaped the postwar global order and has maintained it for fifty years. It has done so almost unconsciously. In the process, it has established a system grounded in the widespread American presence and influence around the world, and that system has set the framework for handling international relations and for finding solutions to global problems.

It matters little what that order is called. Critics of U.S. foreign policy have pejoratively called it the "Pax Americana"; others, more positively, have called it the "Free World." Many of its component principles, such as human rights, financial coordination, non-proliferation of nuclear weapons, or the wide array of international organizations that address world-wide humanitarian, technological and economic issues, are so widely accepted as part of the normal functioning of the world that the importance of U.S. sponsorship and support for them is not perceived or appreciated.

Other elements of American influence, such as the world-wide stretch of U.S. bases, the impact of U.S. deterrence and defense, or the global spread of such American concepts as environmentalism, are often so taken for granted as manifestations of the American role that their effect is not separately understood. But they are the long-term results of U.S. attitudes and U.S. policies, as the American superpower has shaped the world in its own image or in the image of its ideals, principles, and interests.

The influence of that system is so pervasive that even those who oppose it appeal to the principles that it espouses, and so powerful that even the Soviet Union and the Peoples Republic of China must now decide how to join it or adjust to it.

The Federal Republic has fitted into that system from the days that it first obtained U.S. protection. It has fitted into the separate structures, whether NATO, the G-7, or international agencies. It has played a role of growing importance.

As American power and determination wane and its ability to manage the global system declines, the system will have to change. States like Japan or the Federal Republic, or organizations like the European Community, will have to consider what they want to support and what they want to change to their own preferences.

But such changes are not to be taken lightly. The countries that are to shape the new order need to know what they want. The United States and the Federal Republic must decide on their respective future roles.

For a long time, the United States led and Germany followed. Then they worked together, with the United States having the lead. Next, the Federal Republic will play a bigger role. But Bonn is by no means certain that it wants to lead, even if it is no longer ready to follow. And the United States is far from ready to follow, or even to give up leadership, although it often speaks in those terms. One of the reasons for German-American tension lies in their uncertainty about the new roles they will play.

Bonn, Frankfurt, Washington and New York also need to cooperate to sustain the long cycle of prosperity. They need to agree with Brussels, Tokyo, London, Paris, and others, perhaps one day even with Moscow. And, if that prosperity should end, they need to cooperate all the more to avoid a deep trough in the world financial and trading system. They will need to modify the system to handle downturns as well as good times, and to cope with a world of constant adjustment and change.

A Parting or Not?

The events of 1988 and 1989 pose a question that can no longer be avoided: Is there now a possibility, or even a likelihood, of a systemic crisis in German-American relations, one so significant that the two countries might come to a parting of the ways, in which the Federal Republic might give up American protection or the United States might withdraw it?

The fact that many problems that are cited in this book occurred during times when mutually friendly governments were in place both in Bonn and Washington indicate that German-American collaboration has not adjusted to the changes in the power balance between the two states or in the changes in the world around them. Therefore, a crisis cannot be excluded, even if it is not inevitable.

A systemic crisis could come in two ways:

- The first would be a very sharp and even total disagreement about any particular topic in German-American discussions, whether on defense, macroeconomics, arms control, or some other issue that appears particularly urgent at the time. Such a disagreement might be followed by severe mutual recrimination, perhaps by efforts to find a compromise, but it would have changed the tone of the alliance in fundamental ways.
- The second, and more likely, is the death of a thousand cuts, a systemic crisis resulting not from disagreement on any single issue but from a series of minor or major arguments on several elements of the whole range of problems that make up the common agenda, whether in trade, economics, *Ostpolitik,* strategy, or status of forces. Ultimately, they would bring about exhaustion with each other, or a mutual collapse of confidence that would alter the relationship.

In either case, the Germans or the Americans might conclude that they could no longer instinctively look to each other for support.

The near crisis that erupted during the winter of 1988–1989, when Bonn and Washington argued in quick succession about German deliveries to Rabta, Lance Modernization, and SNF negotiations, fell into the second category. Neither capital fully understood the other's needs. They both acted without alerting the other. The Germans were particularly embittered at the accusation that they were following Hitler's policies, just as the Americans were embittered at the implication that they were too militaristic to see opportunities for diplomacy. As luck would have it, there was then no macroeconomic disagreement to help inflame the relationship, although there was a brief test of wills about European Community refusal to import U.S. hormone-fed beef.

The 1988–1989 disagreements were resolved, as others have been in the past. But they had an impact and left political circles in Washington and Bonn wary and uncertain about each other. It is not an experience that either should want to repeat. Neither controls its own domestic dialogue and that dialogue can drive the two countries into greater divergences.

This is, therefore, a sober moment in the relationship. The two countries have to collaborate or at least to understand each other better when they cannot collaborate. It is not an easy task, but it has become an essential one.

The Future Structure

If one wishes to alleviate some of the problems in the relationship, one must recognize that the new objective realities of the relationship will not and should not go away. One cannot wish Europe and Germany to return to 1945 or 1955. One cannot want a return to the darkest days of the cold war. And the United States cannot now be asked to take upon itself again all the burdens of the reconstruction and maintenance of the global order.

What can be done, however, is to improve the conduct of the relationship on all sides. There are measures that can help avoid future crises and that would be especially important over the decade of the 1990s as the two countries attempt to reshape their relationship and also collaborate in bringing about a new Europe and new world.

In that spirit, certain suggestions are in order:

• Senior officials from both countries should explore with each other, and with other NATO states, how they can use a combination of diplomacy and military security measures over the next few years to create a structure that can maintain long-term stability in Europe at lower financial and psychic cost, without risking war, without dissolving the alliance, and without bringing about conditions that would lead to an American withdrawal from Europe or to the neutralization of the Federal Republic.

- Those senior officials should also meet periodically, at least once a year, to discuss major issues of diplomacy, strategy, and economics on a broad basis without being tied to one or another immediate problem. Such consultations would give the two leaderships a chance to talk out their basic approaches rather than to confront each other on separate issues in the hectic atmosphere between flights, editorials, negotiating proposals, or stock market crashes. Instead of discussing details, they could discuss principles.
- They should make a more conscious effort to understand the fundamentals of each other's thinking. They should be prepared to talk more openly and to listen to each other more thoughtfully, not only on individual problems but on the totality of their interests.
- In that respect, they should continue and expand the programs for mutual exchanges and common studies, and the flow of trans-Atlantic visits.
- They should also learn to avoid the kind of inaccurate and tendentious terminology about each other that has all too often crept into their discussions or into their comments to the press.
- Both states and peoples must prepare themselves for another type of relationship than that of the past forty years. The new relationship can and should still be close, even if it cannot and should not remain as it has been for recent decades.
- In economics and finance, as well as in other aspects of a global system, they should begin to work consciously, through trigemony, the G-7, and other structures, toward the foundations of a system that can function over the long haul and under situations of stress.

These steps cannot prevent problems created by genuine differences in national interest or in national attitudes. But they can establish frameworks under which the German-American alliance can prepare itself for the long run. They can also mitigate such problems as do occur, and perhaps lead to better mutual understanding and a calmer atmosphere. They should be able to prevent clashes created by failures to communicate.

The alliance of tomorrow will not be, and should not be, the alliance of yesterday or even the alliance of today. But it can still be a considerable asset to global stability and to the peace and prosperity of both countries. And it can still be a genuine alliance.

If the elements of a new relation are in place, so are the elements of a systemic crisis. Such a crisis could come about by increments, as the alliance began. It need not occur immediately or in one stroke. The basis of the present German-American relationship was established over ten years, from 1945 to 1955. A break could, in the same manner, develop over many years, but at the end the relationship would be significantly altered.

Secretary Acheson wrote of having been "Present at the Creation" of the vast trans-Atlantic dome that has sheltered the Federal Republic and the United States for many decades. It remains to be seen whether we are now present at the dissolution of that which he and others created, or whether changes can be made that will preserve the structure by modifying it. Whichever it may be, Germans and Americans will have to help to shape it, and they will help determine the direction in which the world will go. What they need to decide is whether they will do that separately or together.

Index